G[illegible]'s

NATURE WATCH

Illustrated by the author

HALSGROVE

To Endymion, Robin and Bracken,
three fine country companions

First published in 1998 by Halsgrove

ISBN 1 874448 85 X

British Library Cataloguing-in-Publication-Data
A CIP record for this book is available from the British Library

HALSGROVE
Halsgrove House
Lower Moor Way
Tiverton EX16 6SS
T: 01884 243242
F: 01884 243325
www.halsgrove.com

Printed and bound in Great Britain by
The Devonshire Press Ltd, Torquay

Contents

Preface

By Barrie Williams, Editor of the Western Morning News

Trevor Beer's 'Nature Watch' column has appeared every day in the *Western Morning News* since 1993 and, for many readers, it is the first thing they turn to each morning.

That is hardly surprising, given Trevor's almost uncanny ability to put across his wonderful observations of the natural world in such an appealing conversational style that never fails to inform and entertain.

Trevor is both an expert and an enthusiast for wildlife in all its forms and someone who delights in passing on his enthusiasm to others. He has succeeded in doing that for thousands of *Western Morning News* readers, both through 'Nature Watch' and his other pieces for the newspaper.

This collection serves as a marvellous insight into the beauty and variety of the Westcountry, as seen through Trevor's sensitive and expert eyes. It will delight his growing army of admirers and introduce his splendid work to many more.

Foreword

By Dr Karl P.N. Shuker, zoologist, cryptozoologist and Science writer

Back in the 1960s, as a youngster with a passionate interest in wildlife and reading, I received a goodly number of natural history books as gifts from family and friends. In those days, they often sported titles along the lines of 'Wonders of Nature' or 'Animal Marvels', which skilfully accomplished the decidedly tricky task of presenting detailed, erudite wildlife facts and concepts in an informative but deceptively entertaining manner – so deceptive, indeed, that readers rarely suspected they were being proficiently educated. Such books as these contributed hugely in inspiring me to pursue a career in zoology.

But all things change, and not always for the better. It seems to me that terms such as 'wonders' and 'marvels' have become somewhat unfashionable nowadays when applied to nature. Perhaps they do not sound scientific enough? Certainly, I have noticed a trend lately among wildlife books to adopt what I consider to be an ostentatiously 'ultra-scientific', sterile style of writing in which entertainment is ruthlessly sacrificed in the name of education, instead of realising how much more effective a combination of the two would be.

All too often there is space only for physiology and ecology, evolution and behaviour, with none available for countryside customs and folklore, personal reflection, observations or opinions that dare to veer one iota from the conformist line, and the myriad of unclassifiable but thoroughly fascinating ephemera that can magically transform even the most mundane, abstract 'textbook' subject into one that is suddenly memorable, tangible, and vibrant. Could it be that the gift of writing nature books that inspire as well as instruct has been lost?

Happily, no – as I joyfully discovered when reading this enchanting book. Compiled from Trevor Beer's extremely popular daily 'Nature Watch' column in the *Western Morning News*, it offers the reader a journey into the real natural world, in which the complex intermingling of biological processes, rural traditions, local fables, historical anecdotes, mysteries, musings, and a great deal more are lucidly revealed and celebrated by an expert guide who has spent a lifetime exploring the infinite pathways and byways of nature amid the scenic splendour of the Westcountry.

The lives of so many of our land's most significant animal and plant species and the seasonally changing environment in which they thrive are lovingly encapsulated in the lyrical verbal snapshots that have gained for Trevor such an appreciative audience, both within and beyond the borders of his native Devon, but that is not all. Deftly interwoven within his corpus of hard data, whose details combine scrupulous biological accuracy with disarmingly conversational informality, it is a rich tapestry of legends and lore that charm and delight.

As a townie, I was delighted to unearth such nuggets of rural treasure as hare ghosting, arrows manufactured with bluebell glue, the fabled powers of Jack-go-to-bed-at-noon, the possibility that birds utilise the ancient art of dowsing during migration, the intensely moving spectacle of what would appear to be a bona fide badger funeral, how to obtain crystal wine from crystal trees, why the marbled white was once a half-mourner, the identity of mouldiwarps and brummelty kites, where to find Granny's nightbonnet and dryad saddles, and other surprises far too numerous to list here, ably supplemented by a selection of Trevor's splendid wildlife drawings and photographs.

I can think of no better manner in which to conclude this foreword than to quote a short passage from Trevor's book: 'There is no suffering from boredom if one takes an interest in natural history. A good way to start a youngster off is to instil the sense of questioning and wonderment.' This excellent book will achieve those goals admirably – and not just with youngsters but with readers of any age for whom, like me, the natural world is a world not only of science but also of wonder and marvels. Long may it remain so, and long will it indeed remain so – at least while there are magical books like this one for us to read.

Late Winter

Wet and windy was about the size of it. It was not so bad really on the sheltered side of the hedge and mild enough. It had rained a fair bit through the night and the river was high, running muddy-looking as if a bit surly.

Just downstream a water vole pottered about on a log, shades of *The Wind in the Willows.* I'm very fond of water voles and do not like to hear them called water rats, for rats they are not. It would be close to its nest here for they generally feed close to home, mainly on vegetation but with some worms, water snails and other meat along with the veg.

Strongly territorial, water voles will scent-mark their sites with musk from their flank glands almost daily. In this weather it was barely worth it. If you know how to look it is possible to find the little paths to their regular swimming areas and they are easy enough to observe as they are active around the clock.

Water voles live in complex tunnel systems built into the riverbank with exits above and below water, some several yards in from the river's edge, no doubt in case of sudden flooding.

The breeding season is from late March into September with five or six young to a litter. It is believed that few animals survive a second winter so my little companion of the day may reach the ripe old age of two. She or he looked contented enough, pulling grass up in tiny paws, examining it and dropping it again. Voles really do have a pleasant countenance and I could understand Kenneth Grahame making one a hero of his delightful book.

❄ ❄ ❄

If there can be such a thing as a clump of bats, this was it. In a cave that we'd only looked at in summer before hung a group of horseshoe bats, thirty or more suspended close together near the cave entrance. Greater horseshoes these, in their winter roost. They may well be about on mild days in pursuit of food even at this time of year.

The rule with bats if you come across them unexpectedly, as we had done in this instance, is to leave them well alone and move off. They are very prone to disturbance and indeed are protected by special laws which actually make it illegal to disturb them knowingly. This applies to all our British bats and is a protection they certainly need, for, like so many wild creatures and plants, they have been in decline for some years.

When I was a lad, the lane just up the road from where we lived was a haunt of bats; the dusk skies teemed with them, so much so that you could clearly hear their shrill cries. Back then a pair of barn owls used to come out of a hollow tree that towered over the lane. They would screech and swoop along in the dimness and often catch a bat, or drop into the hedgerow grasses for mice or voles.

Times have certainly changed, not always for the better. Bat and barn owl numbers are seriously down. What a privilege, then, to see these, albeit briefly, then move quietly away and leave them hanging upside down in their chosen roost.

We are strange creatures, usually waiting until a species becomes rare and has to fight for survival before specially protecting it, although we are beginning to wake up a bit.

The foxes are mating now. Their screams in the night can be startling and carry far. As darkness falls and all about is shadow and vague outline a fox scream at close quarters can have a body leaping a five-barred gate.

On several occasions recently I saw a yellowy vixen go into a quarry on my approach, then disappear from sight. The quarry is smallish, probably used for stone for the old barn near by, and for the attractive little bridge over the stream. My collie Bracken would sniff around and then look up and I'd tell him foxes don't fly too well and leave it at that.

About two weeks after the first sighting, after we'd 'lost' her seven or eight times, I looked up as Bracken did and saw the vixen staring me in the eyes from twice my height.

Beside me was a fallen tree and the trunk of this led up to a ledge. Walking away so as not to upset her I found a rise in the ground and scanned the quarry with binoculars. Two holes some six feet apart were along the ledge and from one of these peered the vixen with just her lovely face showing. She was watching Bracken more than me but he was nosing about amongst the trees and oblivious to her.

One earth entrance was bright yellow, the other less so. The vixen was denned up in the site of an old ochre mine. In this area there was quarrying for stone no doubt but also for ochre, one of the earth pigments used in paint-making much sought after many years ago, but no longer dug out hereabouts. Our quarry-dwelling vixen: a self-portrait of a beautiful creature.

❄ ❄ ❄

I have been pondering on bird migration. A dowser who practises his art along ley lines, to find water and other things, I know that animals also follow leys for a variety of reasons, including migration. If birds do follow the earth energy routes that network our planet, do they do it by dowsing? If one thinks about it they have to really. And then I thought, just as we often use instruments to dowse with, what better dowsing rods than the bills of birds?

Consider the thousands upon thousands of migrating birds, leaving homes from all over the world. Pointing their bills towards some far distant shore, they make the vast journeys birds have made for ages, following the 'line' – of what? Earth energy, the largely unacknowledged but very real natural phenomenon that we ourselves can follow, by dowsing.

Dowsing is fascinating. It can be exciting, it can be quite wearing at times. (It's best to practise when there's no one around. I'm sure the middle-aged couple who saw me wandering down a woodland path holding a hazel wand in front of me with two hands thought I'd forgotten my bicycle!) Let's face it, we do not really know what dowsing is, this God-given gift that finds water and minerals and much else besides. It works and that's what is important; we get so bogged down with the 'why' that we miss the joy of what *is*.

❄ ❄ ❄

Dartmoor on a winter's day is a touch bleaker than Exmoor, or maybe it is just that the landscape is more rugged. Certainly the ponies have to be tough in any moorland habitat and the Dartmoor breed must be as hardy as any in Britain.

Dartmoor ponies cover vast distances seeking food. Today we watched a small herd of them clatter across a stream and begin foraging for food along a stone row. By the water's edge two were consuming sedges while the others ate grass, then, moving on, they chewed away at gorse. Gorse was once grown as winter fodder for livestock and was obviously popular with the ponies.

Most of these moor ponies are part-breds and not pure-breds registered with the Breed Society. The pure-breds probably could not take the worst of moorland winters, stud-breds losing some of the hardiness of the moor-bred ponies.

They are beautiful animals. Any nature-watcher frequenting Dartmoor should make a study of them. Their thick winter coats begin to come through in August and remain at least until the following May, such is the environment. Indeed they are excellent barometers. We can learn of impending weather by observing them. Before snow they will become restless and gallop about, moving into the valleys.

Today in the cold sunshine they moved into a craggy area and three of them put their tails against the rocks as if food was no longer a priority. The others moved in closer by them, a sign of a storm on the way. Sure enough, on the horizon, an ominous line of black cloud lay brooding and the wind stirred harder at the grass. It was time to heed the ponies' warning and move on.

A glimpse of movement in the distance through the trees drew my attention. Through the binoculars the movement became two tawny owls, some distance apart on an oak branch. One held a vole or mouse in its hooked beak, facing the other bird, which sidled up to it and took the prey. The first owl backed away and half-spread its wings, watching its partner devour the prize: courtship feeding, one of those rare sights in nature that reward those lucky enough to be in the right place at the right time.

Male tawny owls stake out their breeding territories in November, pairs being firmly established in December. Once the eggs are laid the female deals with the incubation. That is the way of tawny owls but the male has looked after her well by the extra feeding and she is well fortified for the egg-laying.

I have known tawny owl young to be born in January and February in mild winters but a hard cold snap often kills the young ones.

Radar studies have shown that if severe weather conditions alternate between Britain and Europe lapwings, for example, will commute back and forth across the Channel several times in a winter. Such conditions also bring exotic immigrants. Waxwings and crossbills are but two species which will arrive here in large numbers.

So it's important to keep putting out peanuts, 'bird puddings', sunflower seeds and boiled potatoes.

❄ ❄ ❄

Although it is impossible to choose a favourite bird, I do find dunnocks especially cheering when I see them about, be it in the garden or in the countryside. Quietly coloured and going gently about its business, the dunnock is a charming bird, often unnoticed due to its unobtrusive plumage and habit.

Frequently called the hedge sparrow, and the accentor, it is not a sparrow at all. It spends most of its time on the ground under cover of dense vegetation but does frequent bird tables for food. It is best identified by its warm brown upper parts striped with black; the head and underparts are a soft slate grey, the flanks having darker streaks. Look for the narrow beak of the typical insectivore which is quite unlike that of a sparrow.

Dunnocks lay beautiful blue eggs in a nest built fairly low down in dense vegetation.

The setting for one of the most vivid memories I have involving dunnocks was a wood, where my attention had been drawn by a cuckoo which was about to lay in a dunnock's nest. The two adult dunnocks were calling incessantly 'sesseessessees' in obvious alarm as they flitted about close by. Then, from the trees near by and totally without warning hurtled a female sparrowhawk, taking the cuckoo clean off the nest as it was about to settle.

Raptor and prey were gone. No cuckoo's egg had been laid and the dunnocks returned to their posts, the female to incubate the eggs, the male to hold territory near by with his rather rapid song. He would help her with feeding the young as soon as they were hatched. In summertime dunnocks eat mainly insects but now, in winter, plant food dominates the menu. (There cannot be many instances of a sparrowhawk doing another bird a favour!)

Early Spring

Along the shoreline nine little birds sometimes ran, sometimes flew before us: ringed plovers, short-billed, stocky little birds, smartly plumaged with a black collared throat on a white and grey-brown body.

Ringed plovers always appear cheery little birds as they scamper on orange legs along shore and estuary mudflats, but their lot is not so cheery. They nest on shingle beaches above the tideline, a brilliant bit of evolution in that their eggs, beautifully camouflaged to be virtually invisible among the variously hued pebbles, appear to be safe from most predators. But not from mankind.

Our own seeking of peaceful places for countryside walks leads us more and more to wander wild places at all times of the year. Early spring along a shingle beach is a lovely time and place. But it is also the breeding time for the ringed plover and our peaceful thoughts do not lighten the tread of our footfalls upon scrunching shingle.

The birds have one ploy that works well enough with predators: they feign injury. Scrambling away from the nest site with trailing wing they will desperately try to lure an enemy away. The hunter, intent on its prey, often is lured away and then the plover takes wing and escapes, so saving itself and its eggs.

We are not the hunter. We love the little bird scampering away across the beach. And so often, unaware of its ways, and totally unaware of its eggs, we wander on along the beach, near its nest.

We cull the foxes that prey on terns at their nesting sites, yet the foxes are seeking food in their own way. Shall we have to stay away from vulnerable sites rather than cause a decline in a species or should we just be more aware, more careful?

* ❀ *

Surely one of the most extrordinary and moving stories in all nature is that of the emperor penguins and their struggle for survival in the frozen

Antarctic. We cannot imagine temperatures of 70 degrees below zero. Nor can we imagine going for 115 to 200 days without food, which is the ordeal the male emperors have to undergo while watching over their single eggs.

Life In The Freezer was an amazing series and what TV should be about. Reading about wildlife in the Antarctic is amazing enough but to see, even at at second hand, the lives of the Weddell seals and the emperor penguins unfold before our eyes is awe-inspiring. Having gone away to feed, the returning females walk a hundred miles across the ice, to find their mate and chick waiting for them. Then the starving males leave on their own hundred-mile journey to find food, their first for almost four months. I found it astonishing. But then, nature is astonishing, and extremes are all the more so.

A few days ago I was by the river chipping gulls and lapwings free from their night roosts. About four or five times each winter it is so cold – even here in the Westcountry – that birds' feet freeze to the very place they have chosen to sleep in. Once freed they take wing and go searching for food, but not before they circle with shrill cries in a way I am convinced is a thank you for my meagre efforts to help.

Wild creatures know when they are being helped. Being wild, they have to pick themselves up and get on with living. In winter just surviving can be difficult enough.

* ❀ *

The quince in the garden has been in colourful flower since early February, mixing well with a holly tree. Ours has deep pink flowers but some quince flowers are white and the tree is very apple-like.

Introduced into this country from Mediterranean regions, the quince has probably been here since Roman times. It is now a tree of cottage gardens and old hedgerows and produces a fruit midway between an apple and a pear in its irregular shape. The fruit is strongly flavoured and good for jellies, as an additional flavour in apple pies and in preserves, but not as a fruit to be eaten from the trees.

A few years ago two youngsters had their hands over the garden wall scrumping our quinces. I watched them take three or four and then shouted. Off they ran with their loot. I let them go and imagined their triumphant countenances changing once they sank their teeth into the fruit.

Fruit growers use the quince tree as stock on which to graft pears, a closely related tree, and this gives the resulting tree a useful dwarf effect. Quinces fruit in September and October.

After a hard winter the quince usually flowers in April but this year it has been jolly to see the rich pink flowers alongside the gold of jasmine flowers and the deep green of the holly leaves. Blackbirds nest in ours most years. I think the oval quince leaves merging with the holly provide a good rain-proof roof over the nest and the holly certainly deters marauding cats. The early nesters also favour the garden conifers, because the evergreen shelter is constant.

When I see there's a nest in use I place or tie a bundle of fruit netting among the lower branches. That keeps the cats away. In my experience they won't climb into netting, so the birds can go about their business as usual.

Along the middle path the wild daffodils provide splashes of gold against the still wintry looking browns and greens of the wood slope. Last autumn's leaf fall has yet to be pushed aside by this year's vegetation growth, but it is about to happen. A woodcock put up from the slope below the path, gliding silently away and down where the primroses and wood sorrel are always most abundant.

In a steeply sloping woodland like this the rains cause the top-soil to sweep down to form a nutrient rich shelf. Here, the spring flowers are at their best. The bluebells will form a great blue carpet all the way along the top half of the woods, from late April into May.

Our woodcocks stay on. Although many wintering woodcocks move away again for the summer we always have them nest with us very early in the year. Secretive and quiet birds in the main, they are a delight to see. I love to watch them from the cleave of an evening in aerial display, when they chase each other over the marshfield in spurts of sudden activity.

They ground-nest among fallen twigs and leaves, laying in late March or April, and the incubation period is about twenty-three days. The young are on the move very quickly and can fly for short distances at ten days old. The woodcock here quite often lay a second clutch in June.

It is absolutely true that the mother will carry her chicks to safety, held pressed against her belly, if danger threatens. I have been fortunate enough to see this.

A kingfisher speeds upriver and its shrill piping cries seem so loud on a windless morning. Twenty minutes later there it is again, flying in controlled fashion at the riverbank, cutting a tunnel into the mud where tree roots clamber down the bank like gnarled arms reaching for the water below.

So busy was the kingfisher that it was unaware we were some thirty yards downstream of it and we watched for a further ten minutes before a second bird flew by us, called shrilly to say we were seen, and the two flew away high across the meadow. Time to move on. Keep to the rules: never disturb a nesting species, even if it is only the beginnings of a nest.

Along the river in rather bat-like flight came our first sand martins of the year, five of them dipping and weaving as they picked up insects whilst on their way to their nesting places. Like the kingfisher, they will nest in a chamber at the end of a burrow in the riverbank, and in a good summer may well raise two broods of youngsters.

The sand martin is the smallest of the European martins and has brown upper parts with white below and a brown breast-band.

I have known the species nest in quarries and claypits where there are pools of water. Birds do tend to nest similarly as a species, but there are many exceptions to the rule, so the texts of field guides are to be read as general rules and nothing more. For example, I discovered kingfishers nesting in an ancient well and have known willow tits in natural nest holes and marsh tits hacking them out. Both the latter species have nested in my nestboxes on occasions.

These oddities of nature makes observing all the more exciting. There is always something new around the next corner.

* ❀ *

In the town, near the ancient Pannier Market, grew the plantain, stubbornly hanging on to its existence as thousands of human feet either trod on it or missed it by inches.

I could almost feel it flinch as vehicles that should not be in this part of town reversed and argued their way along a street built more for horse-drawn carriages than carbon monoxide spewing tons of metal.

Yet here it was. This great plantain, which would have been happier in some quiet country field, is one of the six species in the British isles; five are native.

This plant is so resistant to injury and bruising that it was thought to be useful against those very problems in people. It was widely used medicinally against bruises and sores. It is still gathered for feeding cage-birds, along with groundsel, and birds actually do love the seeds of this plant.

Another species, ribwort or black plantain, is very common in this part of the country and is very rich in vitamins and minerals. This plantain could be a most useful fodder plant; sheep and cattle will certainly eat it. As the leaves remain on the plant through the winter one would think it a highly prized foodstuff. The problem is that modern weedkillers are made to destroy all broad-leaved weeds, no matter whether they are useful or not.

Along with cow-wheat, it is an important food plant of the rare heath fritillary butterfly, so while we may not find some plants useful another creature does. In many cases such plants are vital to their survival!

It is very humbling to stand and gaze at, say, the food plant of a butterfly – perhaps nettles or the scabious flower – and think, were it not for you a species of butterfly would disappear from this planet. Would that we were so useful and important.

* ❀ *

One of the most exciting moments of springtime is the sight of the first pied flycatcher arriving at the Sanctuary for the summer. Usually they arrive during the last week of April. The males arrive first, their black-and-white plumage showing against the woodland greenery.

By now some of the nestboxes will have been taken by blue and great tits so there is often a kerfuffle if a pied flycatcher chooses a box already in use. Some tense moments can develop and feathers may fly, but I have put up more boxes than are needed and everyone sorts themselves out all right in the end.

Female pied flycatchers are brown and white so it is easy to observe the ways of the two sexes and how they spend the day. Often the male will keep a good eye on an intruder, calling to warn his mate and even lead her back to the nest as a sort of guard, chirping to her all the while.

Seven beautiful clear blue eggs are the usual clutch, with sometimes eight being laid. Usually at the Sanctuary we have six or seven pairs of this species in the boxes, so we count ourselves very fortunate.

They use far less moss than the tits do in nest-building, preferring instead dry oak leaves as support for eggs and young. The adults are good parents; we have lost young only when a few days of heavy rain meant that insect food was unavailable soon after hatching. We have had two or three wet summers and it is nerve-racking to watch the hapless parents endeavouring to find enough food to keep the youngsters and themselves alive in lashing rain.

At least well-maintained nestboxes give adults and young a dry and snug shelter.

Spreading across the old stone wall along the bottom path, ivy-leaved toadflax with its delicate trailing stems has established itself. From now through to September it will be in bloom, its small lilac and white flowers similar to those of snapdragons.

History tells us the plant was introduced here in the seventeenth century. Like all introductions, it knew it was on to a good thing living in Britain and wandered off from rock gardens everywhere to explore the countryside via stone walls and rocky places. Gilbert White planted ivy-leaved toadflax at Selborne in 1779 and refers to its progress there in his naturalist's journal.

Natural history tells us the long stalks carrying the seed capsules curl away from the light, seeking dark shady crevices in which to deposit their seeds, and then on the plant goes, establishing itself throughout the country, though it is rare in northern Scotland.

A very attractive little plant, it is ideal around rocky garden pools, always cheery and in flower through spring and summer. Such stony habitats are preferred by the plant and it is particularly resistant to drought.

Westcountry names tell of its habit: creeping Jenny, mother of thousands, nanny goat's mouths, rabbits, roving Jenny and roving sailor, and many more.

Where next for this lovely plant? It will hang on wherever it can, probably wandering back into gardens where people can afford stone walls. The age of post and wire fencing and wooden fences will not favour its migration. However, for anyone doing a natural history project such a plant in their area would reward investigation.

The lovely bluebell, held back by the cold and wet of a winter and spring that have played havoc with lambing and potato crops, is doing its best to carpet certain woodlands once again.

Obviously, there are good years and bad years for most plants and animals in terms of abundance and much of it is down to climatic conditions.

The bluebell has many lovely local names, such as harebell, pride of the wood, fairy bells, goosey-gander, crow flower and Granfer Greggles. Some can confuse it with other flower species. Cuckoo flower, for example, is a name given to the bluebell and to lady's smock and one or two others. The Scots often called the harebell bluebell, the Scottish flower having paler, less curved petals.

I well remember people cycling with huge bunches of bluebells, primroses and daffodils tied to their handlebars when I was a lad, not just to cheer the home but to hawk from door to door to make a bob or two. Thankfully, this practice seems to have died out. Wild daffodils are a rarity now, probably due to the overpicking, but it was the tramping down of the leaves of the bluebells which destroyed so many, not the actual picking of the flower. Treading the leaves prevents the plant from manufacturing its food, so it is important to keep to the pathways when walking in bluelbell woodlands.

There doesn't seem to be much herbal use made of the bluebell but the slime makes a really good glue and was used in the making of arrows at one time. Rather nice, that; it sort of takes the edge off being struck by an arrow if one knows it's held together by bluebell glue.

* ❀ *

The pink flowers of lady's smock and pink purslane told of a wet meadow. In one area I could just glimpse water lying with the grasses, virtually hiding it.

When I was a lad, the farmer here would dam the stream in dry summers to flood the field to green up the grass. In those days real summers were an annual occurrence. We knew long, hot days would follow each other during the school holidays. If we boys were caught damming the stream the prize was a clip round the ear and a chasing out. Little has changed here since those days, with cattle and sheep farming continuing, along with a good wildlife situation.

Here we call lady's smock cuckoo, milkmaids, lonesome lady, meadow pink, laylocks (lilacs) and naked ladies. Usually a beautifully delicate pink, occasionally white, it is a plant long associated with milkmaids and their smocks. It is also said that the name lady's smock is a reference to the Virgin Mary's smock, found by St Helena in the cave at Bethlehem.

As well as being a watermeadow, the field was also crossed by an ancient pack-horse route to several mills. The hollow way, formed by many years of plodding feet, is a mist hollow in the evenings and from a hilltop it is possible to see the whole route as a ghostly pathway through the valley – visible history.

These meadows and the surrounding landscape tell us about mankind's use of the countryside. Old mill leats dug to carry water from the natural waterway to the great waterwheels that turned the mill machinery. Stone walls, barns and lovely little bridges, all built from the stone from small quarries dotted all about. So much to learn from our ancestors' way of life.

* ❀ *

We had been watching a pair of goldcrests building their nest in a holly tree. Hanging would be a better word perhaps, as the nest is suspended basket-like from a branch, more often in conifers. The nest is an intricate affair of spiders' webs, moss and shreds of wool lined with feathers. To be able to observe them building it was a treat.

The goldcrest is Britain's smallest bird, seven of its eggs equalling its own body weight. The bird is basically green in colour, a lovely, delicate green with paler underparts, double wing-bars and prominent black, yellow and flame crests. They will lay seven to ten eggs in a clutch and are usually double brooded, that is to say they may raise two families in a summer.

As we watched the two birds flitting to and fro with nest material, a blue tit from a nearby nestbox flew into the holly tree and was immediately met by two vigilant and angry goldcrests. The bluetit was merely searching for food, but the tiny $3\frac{1}{2}$-inch birds were strongly territorial and it did not stay to argue.

In nature, real fighting, the harmful beak and claw stuff, is quite rare. Birds and other animals know that injury can so often prove fatal and much of the noisy aggression one witnesses is usually just a threat.

More times than not an intruder will leave a defended territory and move on. Often they have intruded inadvertently so there is nothing to be gained by fighting. As for the occupier, it has a job to do, defending home, spouse and youngsters with a few well-chosen calls of warning. Once the point is made, and the intruder signals its understanding, ruffled feathers are preened and all is well with the world again.

* ❀ *

Since last April the lovely flowers of sweet woodruff have bloomed in the same woodland corner where I have known them since I was a lad.

Always flowering just after the wood anemones, these little white flowers with their neat collars of ruffs of leaves around the stem like green stars seem to appear from nowhere.

Woodruff and wood sorrel, primroses and violets all here together provide a continuity that is reassuring to the nature lover who is concerned about vanishing wildlife.

A huge oak that I used to sit beneath as a lad now lies across the woodland floor, mossy and still beautiful. I sit on its sunlit bole watching a blackbird scuff up the leaf litter in that noisy way they have. If left here, as it should be, the great tree, just an acorn some 250 years ago, will be the home for hundreds of other creatures and plants over the next century or so as it gradually returns to its native soil. And the woodruff will still grow in the corner of the wood, by the stile leading in from the adjoining fields.

Ladies-in-the-hay, lady's needlework and rockwood are some of the old names for woodruff. Garlands of the flowers used to be hung in churches. The plant has the sweet smell of newly mown hay as it dries and was stuffed into pillows, placed among linen and even put into wine. An important plant in country homes, it was also used to treat headaches and melancholy, colds and consumption. Woodruff tea is delicious.

To see it here in its favourite corner of the woods, where it enjoys the afternoon and evening sunshine, should shift anyone's melancholy. To contemplate wild flowers and trees more closely is a gentle way of getting back to nature that works wonders for a body.

I love the field maple. Even its Latin name, *Acer campestre*, has a ring about it. It is also known as English maple, which is a bit naughty, for it occurs in Wales and, less commonly, in Scotland as well. Local names include maplin, dogwood, field oak and whistlewood.

A true native of Britain, it is a superb tree in hedgerow and woodland. I have planted scores of them and it is a joy to wander and see the results of a few hours of healthy effort.

Like the sycamore, which is a near relative, the field maple produces 'keys' or winged seeds similar to ash seeds, although more pendulous. Usually this tree remains an inconspicuous bush but when fully grown it can attain a height of twenty to forty feet.

Country folk used to fashion the hard, fine-grained timber into fancy pipes and snuff boxes and the 'mazar', a wooden drinking bowl or goblet, was made from it. The Welsh have chosen the field maple as the timber for bowl and spoon making for decades and it certainly polishes well. A harp made from this maple wood was unearthed when a Saxon barrow was excavated in Berkshire and the famous Sutton Hoo treasure included a maple Saxon harp.

I know one fine example in some ancient woodland which has a trunk about two feet thick and at the moment song thrushes are nesting deep within its green shelter. The male sings its heart out each day, especially around sunset. A regular evening duet between this bird and a nearby robin, with a distant blackbird joining in as the backing voice, makes for a perfect evening.

* ❀ *

Late on the wing a queen wasp zoomed by, a black and golden insect carrying a strip of wood, and I lost sight of her in the hedgebank. She is pregnant, and busy nest-building. The wood strip will be mixed with saliva to make 'wasp paper' and this will be fixed in position to the roof of the nest until, gradually working from top to bottom, the round golden nest is complete.

The queen has hibernated all winter in some sheltered spot. Now she will construct a comb inside the nest, a comb of many cells, and inside each cell she will lay an egg, fixing each with a glue-like substance.

When the larvae hatch the queen will feed them pieces of flies and continue to nest-build. When ready to pupate each larva will spin a silken sheet to seal the end of its cell. About five weeks after the eggs were laid, fully grown wasps will bite their way out. These are the worker wasps. The queen's work is now done. The workers will seek food and expand the nest, building on many new cells, while the queen is busy with full-time egg-laying.

The workers feed the larvae as they hatch. The colony increases rapidly and may eventually contain up to five thousand wasps. The nest may eventually be the size of a football.

In August the males and young queens leave the nest and mate to ensure there will be pregnant queens for the next season. Once mating is over the queens will go off to seek winter quarters and the males, or drones, die.

Worker wasps will then kill and eat any remaining larvae, destroy the nest and leave it, soon to die themselves, as will the old queen, come the autumn cold and damp. A strange but efficient way of life.

* ❀ *

I wonder how many of the people who visit the seaside at this time of year will notice the beauty of the plants that live on the tidal saltmarshes. It is wonderful habitat type. Much of it is covered twice daily by the mix of salt and fresh water and positively zoned by the action of waves, splash areas and such.

Mostly the flowers of these saltmarshes appear from July onwards but now is a good time to look and to brush up on your knowledge of them in readiness for the summer.

Sea lavender and sea purslane are fairly common, the first having lovely rosettes of bright green leaves and blue flowers. It is popular with flower arrangers for winter decorations. Sea purslane is nothing like the pink purslane now on show in our damp meadows. The seaside plant has minute green flowers and the whole plant appears to be covered in a grey 'flour'. *Halimone* it is called, from the Greek for 'daughter of the sea', which is an apt name because the plant is entirely covered by most high tides.

Look for sea milkwort between now and August. The flowers have no petals but the bell-shaped calyx is divided into five pink, petal-like segments.

And what of the seaweeds? A closer look at these rewards the seashore wanderer, for they vary a great deal in form and colour and many are strikingly beautiful. All seaweeds are algae. They are divided into four main groups, according to colour: the blue-greens, greens, browns and reds. Once they were very valuable as a manure and a foodstuff and used especially on coastal farms. Laver, of course, is a well-known food often on sale in fresh fish shops and is excellent fried with bacon and mushrooms. Lovely stuff, but to be eaten only when there is an 'r' in the month, remember.

The middle path in the woods is ideal for bird-watching. The woods are on a fairly steep slope and it has good views over the whole area of oaks, beeches, ash and other trees.

Oddly enough, two of the 'quieter' birds are most obvious at present and both are flycatchers. Seven pairs of pied flycatchers are nesting in boxes and I found two more visiting tree holes higher up in the canopy areas.

The spotted flycatchers are also 'in' but do not use the boxes, preferring instead the crevices and ivy creepers, where they build their nests in well-hidden spots. This is the better-known species of flycatcher, more widespread across the country and quite happy to nest in gardens, even in porches, hanging baskets and the like. They seem to follow in after the pied flycatchers, often coming with the swifts in early May when the pied has already begun nesting.

Both species may produce second broods, although in my experience this is rare and the pieds certainly have not over the past three wet summers. With heavy rainfall in the summer, birds have a hard enough time of it feeding one brood and themselves.

Another summer visitor here in the wood is the redstart, one of the ‘chats’ along with the stonechat, whinchat, robin, and wheatear. In fact the nightingale is also in this grouping.

The redstart, too, has chosen a nestbox in which to lay eggs and raise its young. They are notoriously shy birds and slip into cover when anyone approaches. Often just the flick of the bright, almost scarlet tail is the only clue of its presence. It is this wonderful tail that gives the bird its name, *steart* being an old English word for ‘tail’.

* ❀ *

Pimpernels are lovely little flowers, often as elusive as their name suggests to most of us.

Old man’s weatherglass, shepherd’s sundial and Jack-go-to-bed-at-noon are other names for the scarlet pimpernel, which was once used against toothache, snakebite and kidney and liver disorders. It is a delight to see in open ground. The flowers open around 8 am and ‘go to bed’ around 3 pm, which makes it a popular plant to include in herb clocks in the garden. They also close in dull weather. I once found scarlet pimpernels with both red and blue flowers on the same stem and they are sometimes to be found white- and lilac-coloured.

In Ireland it is a blessed herb and is claimed to have the power to move against a stream. Held in the hand it reputedly gives second sight and the holder can also understand the speech of animals and birds.

Fairly common in uncultivated places, it is a pretty little plant, related to the much less common pink bog pimpernel, which is losing ground to drainage and cultivation.

The yellow or wood pimpernel is called the star-flower in the West-country and Mary’s clover in Ireland. The yellow flower’s healing qualities include the power to alleviate pain though its cousin, creeping Jenny, was more popular with herbalists and with gardeners, who still use it to cover old stonework or the edges of ornamental ponds.

The flowers contain no nectar or scent so are rarely visited by insects. It is likely that the name pimpernel comes from *bipinella*, a diminutive of the Latin *bipinnis,* meaning ‘two-winged’ and a reference to the plant’s leaves.

Now is the time to look for all these delightful flowers. In fact the generic name for the scarlet and bog pimpernels, *Anagallis*, means ‘delightful’, I believe.

* ❀ *

On a mild evening recently I saw a host of buttercup-yellow spiders, scores of them, clustered all around the old gate-fastener and the outdoor tap in the garden. Opening the gate disturbed them. (If you can open a gate, that is: I read somewhere that gate is Old English for 'the way through', the hole and not the stopper, as it were). As the spiders gradually reassembled following the disturbance, looking closely I could see the dark patch on the hind part of their globular yellow abdomens.

These were the spiderlings of the garden spiders and their family life would soon cease. Just as well, really. Choosing gate-fasteners and the area around the top of a tap does not seem too bright as they are constantly in use.

It is a golden time of year altogether, just as there are purple times and white times in the countryside. Now tormentil, bird's-foot trefoil, yellow flag, dandelion and buttercups are everywhere and the gorse is wonderful.

All three common species of buttercups – furious, biting herbs, they have been called – are known as crow-toes, gilty cups, crazies, goldcups and fairy basins in the Westcountry. Cattle wandering a buttercup meadow on a sunlit evening are a lovely sight. It was well known that you had to rub buttercups on cows' udders to ensure good butter-making, and it was thought that the fairies sprinkled cows' hooves with the pollen. Many of us have tilted a buttercup flower under a girl's chin to see if it reflected gold and she liked butter!

That beautiful member of the buttercup family, the water crowfoot, now graces our waterways.

More rain. What do birds do when it's wet and windy, or at night? This is never mentioned in the field guides, although hundreds of books now tell us about their habitats, nests, eggs, young, identification and so on. The secret lives of wild creatures can differ greatly across just a few species.

The robin in the garden is a good place to start. Territory is a great part of a robin's life, particularly that of the male. Robins fighting are likely to be arguing over territory. These disputes can be vigorously aggressive, but usually the 'incoming' robin, who may be exploring new territory, is the one to move on.

The cock robin's pleasantly sweet warble can be heard almost all the year round and is a reminder of a claim to territory. The 'tic-tac' call often heard is an alarm call and may tell of a cat or other intruder in the vicinity.

Roosts are usually in the denser herbage or shrubs and quite well chosen, away from the prevailing wind and often beneath an umbrella-like branch of greenery which staves off most of the rain.

Nests are rarely used again once the young have fully fledged but in the garden here a robin regularly roosts under an old blackbird's nest. If a second clutch follows on quickly from the first in the breeding season, the male may well take over the feeding and care of the first brood until they are independent and then assist the female with the second. In the Westcountry breeding often begins in March, whereas in the North it may be delayed until June.

* ❀ *

In a way the nests of the willow warblers and chiffchaffs, set in ground hollows as they usually are, can be likened to little houses. They seem so vulnerable, but the birds have built in this way over the centuries and surely must know their business.

In the herbage by the middle path a gold- and brown-marked leaf-shape moved and in moving announced itself as a frog exploring the woods. Its expressive eyes watched me and then off it went in leisurely manner into the woodrushes which thrive here.

Somewhere young frogs will be dispersing, tailless now, their tiny feet propelling them through grassy fields and across traffic-laden roads where so many perish, never making the journey into adulthood. Most travel by night or in the early morning, seeming to know the perils of the roads.

It is in their nature to migrate now, but in just a score of years times have changed dramatically: the motor vehicle that serves our needs and provides us with a deal of pleasure in being able to get to interesting places also means the end for so much wildlife.

On a tree trunk several flies perch bat-like, upside down. These are *Heptis scolopacea*, or the oak fly, which I know as the downlooker from chatting to anglers, for it is a good trout fly. They always seem to perch head down, standing high on their front two legs. Perhaps it helps when they drop away to fly, a quicker, more effective starting position.

Flies deserve more of our interest. Some are stunningly beautiful and not all are health hazards. Many do really useful work in the countryside.

* ❀ *

Aren't oak trees wonderful? Well, all trees are, but oaks are pretty special in that they play host to much more life than most other species. For example, more insects are dependent on oaks than on any other tree species. They have been around a long time, of course, and at this time of year the caterpillars of some 110 species of butterfly and moth alone have been found on the oak.

Birds love oaks, too. They provide home, shelter and food all in one tree for some species: the total habitat. I watched a treecreeper in a wood recently and though it did move from one oak to another it stayed with the species and eventually went back to its roost, behind bark in one of the older oaks in the wood. The great tree would shelter it for the night and at dawn they would begin another busy day together.

Lower in the wood, its spotted coat blending with the sun-dappled vegetation all around, a young red deer gazed along the path taken by its mother. Large dark eyes watched and waited, knowing she was feeding somewhere deeper in the wood, soon to return to their hideout among the friendly trees to feed her baby.

Summer Days

Open field country and the man-made patchwork farmland with small spinneys and copses are very much part of the English scene, the patchwork in this area made by the hedgerows.

The 'little bit of bread and *no* cheese' call of yellowhammers is loud and far-carrying here, the species liking the fairly open habitat with trees. One misses the elms, though. One of the sad landmarks of our recent rural past is the loss of these beautiful trees, which were so much a part of the scene up to the 1970s. I always thought of yellowhammers, elms and certain butterflies as a special part of my boyhood. Some remain, of course. The yellowhammers are nesting in an old hedge that was here in Domesday times, though the name Domesday was coined a mite early and may be fairly seen as more applicable today.

Yellowhammers are yellow buntings, glorious bursts of golden sunshine as they flit about in the greenery, the males particularly striking with their bright-yellow heads.

By the river among the alder trees a reed bunting, a cousin of the yellowhammer, calls continuously. The two species' habitats overlap here, thanks to the slow-flowing river in the valley below.

Buntings are fairly easily observed, especially the males, who perch conspicuously and call away in the breeding season, enabling birdwatchers to get a good view of them.

As both these species tend to have two and sometimes three broods in a year, the breeding season is spread nicely across the spring and summer months, nicely that is for nature-watchers who enjoy sitting under a tree and seeing it all happen around them.

For a while now it has been glow-worm time. These remarkable beetles are around and about in the countryside, quite rare in some places, yet always to be found in others. This year we have found quite a few. The loveliest sight we had of these insects was a group of them in stinging nettles, some shining their light through the green leaves.

On a hillside near a favourite wood we were able to read the writing on the page of my notebook in the glow of their light. The next day I wrote an ode to a glow-worm, and two nights later took it out to read it to them in their own light, just for the fun of it. An eccentric sort of thing to do, but peaceful, fun and different. They must have enjoyed it for they kept their lights on!

Some of the healthier females give off a light powerful enough to illuminate the grasses for an inch or two around themselves. The males will also glow but to a much lesser extent. Occasionally they may switch off – and then burst into green flowing light again in a wonderful manner. To have them in the garden in high numbers would be a treasure, both visually and practically, for they would certainly keep snails in check.

It is ladybird time, too. These are everyone's favourite beetles, with their jolly colours and helpful ways in the garden. Would that they were as plentiful as they once were but, as with so many creatures, we have not helped them as much as they have helped us.

Their colours are a warning to birds that they contain alkaloid poisons and are distasteful and possibly dangerous to eat.

There has been a remarkable increase in slugs this summer. They are blackening the lawns with their evening perambulations. The increase is almost certainly due to the succession of mild winters we have had.

All slugs, and there are more than twenty species in Britain, are hermaphrodites, having both male and female sex organs. After mating, both partners lay eggs, which live through the winter to produce a new generation of slugs in the spring. As individual slugs may live for three years, they stand a good chance of survival and reproduction of their kind.

The great black slug is our largest and most common species. Here in the Westcountry the great grey, the garden slug and the netted or field slug are also common.

Slugs' liking for vegetation makes them pests in our eyes but of course they know nothing of gardens and such and the territories we requisition. We unintentionally provide them with a larder and they unintentionally upset us when they come to supper.

As well as slugs we have snails, some eighty species of them in Britain, and that is just the land snails. Most of these eat plants but some are carnivorous, preying upon other snails and small creatures of the soil.

The garden snail is very common, but so are the white-lipped and black-lipped banded snails, and the spiral-shelled moss snail.

Slugs and snails are well worth studying, just to see which kinds are in the area and, of course, to add to the flora and fauna reports always welcomed by County Wildlife Trust records.

Six am. In the early morning sunshine the woods were palely lit and peaceful. Blackbirds and robins were splashing in a pool near the old well, freshening themselves for the coming day. A sparrowhawk in gliding flight almost sauntered along the pathway about six feet up, its low flight taking it out into the open meadow, sunlit under swift-moving clouds heading towards Exmoor on the sou'westerly wind. Here, between the wood edge and the field, was a mass of great willowherb with just a few plants in flower, yet the promise was there of deep pink flowers in a day or two. A chaffinch family was out and about, a female and four young, with a male calling 'pink-pink' near by.

The chaffinch was once recorded as the commonest bird in Britain, but to my mind there are more greenfinches about these days than chaffinches, certainly in this area. I feel sure there has been a decrease in chaffinches generally, which may be due in part to the use of toxic seed dressings and possibly to the loss of hedgerows in many areas. Habitat loss, that worrying factor facing all living creatures, means more than just the disappearance of habitats; it is about the pollution and poisoning of sites and the food a creature or plant lives on.

The family of chaffinches vanished into the willowherb and I could hear their chattering and see the vegetation sway. They feed mainly on seeds from the ground, and on insects. Their song, though easily identifiable, varies between individuals quite enough to pick out differences and it is said there are distinct 'dialects' in different regions of Britain.

It is good to know the old dialects are being retained by the birds. One hopes people will retain theirs too.

Two field voles were chasing each other around the bole of a tree about three feet from the ground. The tree, an oak at the edge of the wood, gave them easy footing with its rugged bark. I should not have been so surprised to see this, really, if one considers their agility when running up slender grass stems and other vegetation.

It was a warm summer's evening with long shadows and golden light, the voles busy playing, taking insects and improving their network of runs through the field vegetation. They are busy burrowers, too, and for such small creatures they display a most active and positive attitude to enlarging and improving their homes.

They are, of course, a popular prey item for owls, foxes and the like. Even the shadow of a bird flying over will have them scurrying for cover and safety, naturally enough. A touch of in-built wisdom.

In the hedgerow grows valerian, its pink flowers soft and downy looking with a pungent odour that attracts the bees in good numbers. Not as common as I remember, it is a useful plant to treat nervous disorders and epilepsy, best known as a sedative. Dried valerian roots were traditionally used as a protection against moths in chests of clothing. This is safe enough, but one must be extremely careful when using it as a sedative, for an overdose can result in anger and agitation. It is also an effective cure for insomnia, they say. You can mask the strange taste of the valerian root tea with honey.

If you are making up your own herbal preparations be sure that it is *Valeriana officinalis* you pick and not red valerian, *Centranthus ruber*, which makes nice salads and soups, but lacks the medicinal properties.

It is a sad fact of life that house martins do not seem as welcome as they once were, nesting under the eaves of houses. This summer some have been attempting to build at their usual nest sites day after day, only to have their nests swept away.

I saw a lovely old farmhouse in a very rural part of Exmoor absolutely festooned with strips of polythene sheeting, all swinging in the wind to keep the house martins at bay. Quite right, one might say – it is up to each of us to do what we choose and to make our own progress and mistakes in life – but I could not help wondering at the eyesore of the plastic strips as opposed to a few bird droppings. There was so much plastic flapping about it almost required planning permission.

Anyone with half an eye to the countryside knows that we do not have the numbers of martins, swallows and swifts swooping across our skies that we used to. Such a wonderful sight and part of summertime they were, and still can be.

The young ornithologist today will happily exclaim: 'Oh, there's a swift flying over!' If they but knew it, just a few decades ago the skies were black with them, and with swallows and martins, and there was a bird's nest in every few yards of hedgerow, and such things as elm trees.

Chemicals, science's answer to all ills, for improved food production, pesticides and herbicides, drugs and such, are all polluting our planet. I maintain that the decline in various wildlife species we are witnessing is but a marker and a warning to mankind as a species.

The buzzard flew low over the cornfield, now stubble and glistening wet after rain. The bird was carrying a rabbit, a fully grown animal, which was probably why it was finding it difficult to gain height. About mid-field it dropped to the ground with its prey and ate steadily for about five minutes, then grasped the rabbit again and flew off, higher and higher until it was lost from view among the trees.

Bracken looked up at me and smiled. He wanted to go into the woods too. A mass of trees must spell heaven to a dog.

The buzzard incident had its thought-provoking side. Had the raptor needed a meal to gain strength, the more easily to lift its prey, or had it reasoned that to lighten the load by eating some would help? (Though that would be more like distributing the weight than lightening it.)

Birdsong has more or less ceased now and is sadly missed. To be fair, a chiffchaff and a willow warbler were singing, not yet giving in to the season's end, their songs cheering the somewhat less than summerish day.

In the woods a badgers' sett showed signs of fresh activity, the earth spread about the entrances and gullies in front of the holes telling of badgers and not foxes here. Foxes discard their excavated soil in a fan-shaped ramp immediately below an earth entrance and the two types of homes are fairly easily to identify even for the beginner.

As we crouched to get a better view of the sett a fox appeared over the hedgebank, a typical foxy grin on its face, looked into Bracken's eyes to find the dog was smiling back at him, and vanished.

Young newts in the pond and much activity from adult newts making their undulating way through the water, a joy to see. The ghost of a newt floats pale upon the water, the shed skin of one of the creatures drifting in the current caused by the movements of its former owner.

It is unusual to see an almost whole skin. Usually they are shed in pieces and thus not recognised for what they are. Newts can reproduce a lost limb, too. (Surprisingly, they can also emit a faint but quite audible call.)

Newts retain their tails throughout their lives, unlike frogs and toads, and use them as the chief means of locomotion in water as well as fanning them as part of the mating display, always conducted below the surface.

Here from the surface of the water projected pink flowers of the water-growing form of bistort. There is a land-growing form, *Polygonum bistorta*, which likes damp meadows but the plant here, *P amphibium*, will also grow onto the banks of waterways.

More than twenty years ago, *The Times* newspaper promoted a contest for puddings made from bistort leaves, advertising it as a world championship contest. Bistort pudding, or Easter-ledge, as it is called, is still popular in Yorkshire and the Lake District.

Bistort root contains a high level of tannin, used for tanning leather. It also has astringent properties and was once used for arresting internal and external bleeding as well as treating toothache and various infectious diseases.

What hidden secrets there are in the wonderful world of plants.

The yellow-flowered sow thistles in the garden are eight feet high. They have been splendid this year with two-inch-thick stems. Today the slight breeze lifts the seed heads and the seeds are blowing eastwards. Hopefully some will take and flourish.

The plant is sometimes said to increase the flow of milk of sows when they have farrowed (hence its name). Here in the Westcountry it is also called hare's lettuce and milky dickle, milkweed, rabbit's meat and dog's thistle. It is said to give strength to hares when they are overcome with heat.

The creeping thistle is the one that snags our socks and pierces ankles as we wander rough pasture. Its name tells of its two ways of reproduction: by seed dispersal and by means of its creeping root system, which sends up new plants away from the parent plant.

Difficult to eradicate, it is a tough plant in field or garden and resistant to weedkillers. It is also a good butterfly plant, the flowers having a pleasant musky odour which attracts insects including migrant species such as the painted lady. Butterflies are its usual pollinator and in mid-summer fields it is not uncommon to see many species associating with the thistle.

The painted lady is a very attractive butterfly, a sort of mix between a small tortoiseshell and red admiral in colour and markings. They migrate to Britain from south-western Europe and North Africa and are said to fly at speeds of ten miles per hour.

When seen on the wing in September they will be from the second generation, that is, from eggs laid here by early migrants. None are likely to survive our cold winters.

'Just the weather for ducks,' people say when it is raining hard. We assume that water-living animals like the rain more than we do, yet if you look carefully it is 'Mad dogs and Englishmen', who go out not only in the sun but in the pouring rain.

It is very pleasant occasionally to walk in the rain, especially summer rain, which can be soft and warm. Not so, however, a few days ago. We had just arrived on Braunton Marshes to be greeted by a downpour which swept in off the estuary at surprising speed. Mallards and moorhens ran for it, the moorhens literally running on the water to gain the shelter of the little bridges scattered about this fascinating area of man-made dykes and reclaimed tidal land.

Dusty tracks immediately became yellow mud. Beetles, caught unawares by the sudden downpour, swept by or whirled in little pools, legs waving. We stopped to rescue a score or so but in such a vast area it was almost fruitless to try. Still, a few may remember being hoisted from water and set safely beneath overhangs of bank where miniature 'caves' were dry and welcoming.

Telling my companions to watch their footing, I fell off the steep bank, built here in the 1800s by Dutch and Irish workers, and attempted to bounce nonchalantly back onto my feet and resume our conversation all in one movement. Not so easy as it used to be, so I settled for an undignified mallard-like scramble. We decided to abandon the site meeting. At least I now matched the landscape exactly, good camouflage.

Only cattle remained stalwartly braving the onslaught of rain. They had no choice. In the village the rain ceased. People came out of doorways tidy and dry, staring at four very dishevelled, bedraggled, wet and muddy creatures of the wilds.

Almost luminous in the evening light and one of the largest of all British wild flowers, the hedge bindweed was everywhere along the wood edge, climbing trees and lower vegetation. The pure white trumpet-like flowers seem better this year than for a long while. Rope-bind, some call it, probably because of its persistence in remaining when it likes a place.

The flower shape gives it the lovely country names of granny's night-bonnet and lady's shimmy; the whiteness, Daddy's whiteshirt; and its creeping and climbing habit the names creeping Jenny, Jack-in-the-hedge and Robin-run-the-hedge.

Though they close in dull weather the flowers will stay open all night if there is a goodly moon and the plant certainly earns another of its country names, morning glory, when seen at dawn.

Look carefully and you will see it climbs by using its stems, twisting them in an anti-clockwise direction around the support shrub. I have seen them twelve feet up in hawthorn.

No real medicinal use seems to have been found for the plant but maybe it lies in wait to be discovered, as so many must do.

Occasionally one is lucky enough to see the large convolvulus hawkmoth at these flowers. They appear to be scentless yet they attract this moth so perhaps, and surely, there are perfumes in the countryside too delicate for our own senses to detect. The hawkmoth's wingspan is the largest of any British insect and its long probing tongue, at $3^1/_2$ inches (90 mm), helps make it a most impressive insect. It jabs its tongue into the tubular flowers while hovering in front of the plant.

Hundreds of gulls have been seen wheeling in the skies recently, not only in coastal areas but far inland. This is an annual phenomenon caused by the winged ants from all the nests in an area making their first and last flight, during which each queen is fertilised by a male.

The timing is determined to an extent by local weather conditions and the flight may take place any time from mid-July to mid-August. The gulls, made aware of the situation by some local scout, home in on the ants and many thousands are then devoured.

The fertilised queen will return to her old nest or begin a new one. She then either loses or bites off her wings and lays a few eggs. They develop into sterile female workers which the queen feeds with saliva secretions. She will never leave her nest and may lay eggs for some fifteen years, using sperm stored from that initial mating to fertilise them. She need never mate again and will occasionally withhold sperm from an egg, the unfertilised eggs developing into males.

Ants are fascinating creatures. They eat animal and vegetable food and will also attack and kill other insects and generally scavenge. When a foraging worker finds food it will leave a scent trail which other ants will follow. The black ant, *Lasius niger,* is the one most likely to be found in gardens; it feeds partly on the honeydew of aphids. The mound-building ant *Lasius flavus* actually keeps aphids in its nest during the winter and puts them out to graze in spring.

The so-called ants' eggs used as fish food are actually the cocoons containing the pupal stage of the ant.

Half-mourners were about the meadow. After two days of rain the welcome sunshine was hot, the steep grassy slope filled with late summer flowers and these marbled white butterflies.

In the nineteenth century, women wore black and white dresses as half-mourning, following the period of full mourning for a loved one who had passed over, full mourning being all black, of course. The butterfly's name changed from the half-mourner to the marmoris and marmoress (from marmoreal, meaning 'like marble'), and eventually to the marbled white.

A strikingly beautiful butterfly, it is about now and is abundant at the Sanctuary in most years when there is a hot, dry spell. In fact, it is one of the browns and moreover, it is a black butterfly with white spots, not white with black spots, and is well worth closer study.

To do that just sit in a field where the insects are on the wing for they will come close enough to be easily observed. Never take specimens. Leave them be, for they are setting down the next generation while in flight.

Like the ringlet, the marbled white lays its eggs while flying and has only one brood each year.

Its food plants are grasses and the butterfly loves to feed from flowers such as knapweed, scabious, thistles and bird's-foot trefoil.

Look closely and you will see it walks on four legs, not six as do the large and small whites, which as we all know favour cabbage family plants. August will probably see the last of the butterflies for this year. Their passing will signal the coming of autumn and many changes in all we see and hear in the countryside.

With the youngsters on holiday, it's a good time to spend a day or two nature-watching with them on the beach. At first glance the sand looks bare and uninteresting. But look a little more closely. Small tunnels lead into the sand and empty shells are scattered about. Beneath the sand, animals are in hiding protected here from the force of the waves and from drying out.

Look for lugworm burrows. They are U-shaped and one end fills up with sand at high tide. The lugworm eats the sand and a dip or depression forms at the entrance to the burrow as the sand slips down. The sand grains are passed out at the end of the worm and this forms the cast at the other end of the burrow.

Such creatures which live in sand obtain their food from the particles of decaying animals and plant remains mixed with the sand. Thus they consume large quantities of sand, extracting the edible bits and rejecting the sand. The beach is a vast larder (the true original of sandwiches, perhaps).

And watch those wading birds at work, probing with their bills of varied lengths according to species. The bills are sensitive; the birds hunt not by luck but by judgement and feel, the differing lengths of bill exploiting food at differing depths in the sand and mud.

The empty razorshells found on beaches were once home to living creatures. Like the cockles and tellins, these bivalves filter out edible particles from the water or from the sand surface by pumping water through the body. The body has two tubes, like syphons, and the water is drawn into one and pumped out through the other.

Show the youngsters a few things like this and tell them their whole world is filled with such wonders to be explored.

Dew-fall was on the long grass in the meadow. Next month we will see real dew, that is, a lot more than now in late August.

Dewponds are few and far between hereabouts. In some areas dewponds were important as sources of water for both the shepherd and his sheep. Saucer-like depressions some twenty or thirty feet across, they used to be lined with straw and topped with clay, trodden in hard. They collected rain, of course, but the dewfall replenished them regularly, and most were made in shallow gullies just over the brow of the downland so as to catch the continuous flow of sinking moisture-laden air. As air cools and becomes more dense it sinks, causing a noticeable breeze down over some hillsides at dusk. This is why dewponds were built in such places.

Some dewponds are very old, the idea and the observations that spawned the idea were obviously well noted long ago.

The nearest dewpond I know of was made by the landowner for added wildlife interest in his large garden. It was not trodden in. The farmer ran a tractor back and forth a few times and that trod the clay down tight-packed. Now it is a joy to see, teeming with wildlife and with some beautiful plants.

Stand on a hillslope of a late summer's eve and as the sun sets you will notice the subtle change, the little breeze hastening gently down the slope, the slightest bending of the grass stems and then the dew. Toe-caps take on a shine as you walk homewards and the dog's coat clings tighter.

A cock pheasant strutted the hedgerow in resplendent scarlet and bronze, caught in the evening sunlight. He crowed the call of all cock pheasants, the 'going to roost' call also foretelling sunshine on the morrow.

The breeding season over, the pheasant can get on with life now, with only mankind and foxes to worry about. As he was coming up my side of the hedge I assumed he hadn't seen me. Sure enough I was able to watch him come closer, giving occasional pecks at the long grass, then with a clatter of wings he was up into the old oak by the linhay field gate.

Pheasants prefer to roost in trees at night. It's safer up there, and despite their large size they are not easy to see in a tree. I had seen this one fly straight up but it took ten minutes to find it with binoculars, then found it was staring straight at me all the time.

No matter how used to binoculars one becomes it is still disconcerting to look right into the eyes of a wild creature; you feel you are only a few feet distant. I find this with foxes and deer and suppose it is knowing they are well aware of your presence.

With all wildlife-watching, the stalking close and the thrill of getting superb views are part of the excitement, the old hunting instincts coming out even though the intent is different.

The pheasant is our most widespread game-bird but it is not a native. Its natural home is Asia, birds from the Caucasus having been introduced into Britain during the Middle Ages. They did well here, becoming common. In the seventeenthth century, birds from China were introduced, the type we see with the white collars.

There is quite a variety of plumage, some melanistic birds looking unusual in their dark green garb while occasionally one finds creamy white, albinistic birds wandering about.

A cuckoo clearly calling in August must be a rare thing but a cuckoo it was. We watched it fly westwards low over the estuary floodplain; then it rose to fly south and was gone. Was it calling a sort of goodbye to the area it had summered in? There have been few enough cuckoos in recent years and I have missed the calls that used to be so commonly heard.

In fact, despite the breeding season being over, it was a day of bird calls, as is typical of estuarine habitats. A small flock of whimbrel flew in. Again, a bit of a surprise; they seem early, yet there is a spoonbill on the river, so who can make rules on arrival and departure times?

The rapid calls of the whimbrel always carry far and it was a joy to watch their flight silhouettes become larger as they came in over the house-tops and fields to drop to the low-tide mudflats.

Then the oystercatchers started, as noisy as redshanks. Both species act as sentinels, warning of disturbance in good time to send other birds winging away.

Some of the whimbrel had orange tints on the rump, others pure white; family parties on passage probably as the former colouring is that of young birds, the white, of adults.

A long greenshank, its white rump showing clearly, flew by and wheeling to one side dropped into a freshwater marsh, where it immediately began fishing in a pool. There can be few birds which have more wildness about them than this northern breeding species, an elegant wader. The call of a greenshank evokes all the magic of a wild Scottish glen no matter where one hears it. It is as the skirl of the pipes and stirs the heart.

Recent high winds set the scene and the Sanctuary, facing east, caught the brunt of it. Five deer lay in a row behind the bank on the bottom path. They looked up at me from their shelter 200 feet below where I stood as if to say, 'Go away, we live here,' so I went.

Kestrels nested this year in a tree cavity only yards beneath a kestrel box I'd put up. The three young have flown, so the box probably acted as a roof against rain and too hot a sun. Twice I saw the male perched atop it. Maybe next year they will nest inside.

More than three hundred fledglings off the nextboxes this year: tits, nuthatches, pied flycatchers, redstarts ... lovely.

I always clean out our nestboxes around September time, taking care there are no late nesters. In February I recheck them, repair any winter damage, turf out the odd slugs which have taken up residence, and await the first birds at nesting time (usually bluetits).

Birds like to build afresh. Cleaning out the boxes gets rid of nest parasites. Quite a few nestboxes on sale in shops are completely closed, without a hinged lid or other access. I would avoid those, for you cannot clean them out and who knows what may be inside? Sometimes young ones die before fledging and the box is not likely to be used again with carcasses inside. Clean the boxes out, I say.

If you are making a choice between binoculars and telescopes for nature-watching, choose binoculars every time, with 7x to 10x magnification. If a telescope is to be an added piece of equipment, be sure the object lens measures no less than 60 mm, for good light-gathering power.

Silent now save for the little murmuring discussions between themselves, the various warblers are feeding up, preparing for their amazing journeys back to Africa and the Mediterranean. Five leaf warblers, chiffchaffs I would call them, come into the garden from the wood each day. No song now to identify them by, but sometimes a late summer burst, then off they fly.

It is good to think of them when one is journeying into town and taking ten minutes longer than usual because of traffic queues. What a daft lot we are, moaning about such things.

Try putting a cassette of birdsong in the car. Listen to the marvels of Mother Nature caressing the mind; what a beautiful beginning and end to a working day. Shops in the town might try that instead of the babble of music some put out.

The chiffchaffs will fly south about three weeks later than the willow warblers. In fact, they summer with us longer altogether, as they arrive earlier by a couple or so weeks. Although most head for Africa, some stay in southern Europe and, of course, a few do overwinter with us, along with a few blackcaps.

The warblers are mainly insect feeders and so it is not wise for them to stay on here for a winter when insect food is sparse, and in hard weather spells, virtually non-existent.

Follow the leys, follow the sun, find food en route and on arrival: that is the way of life of these little winged nomads.

I was giving a talk the other day to a group of youngsters. One asked how he could enjoy bird-watching 'with too many birds to learn about'. Why not choose a family of birds such as the warblers or crows and study them in all their habits and habitats?

Autumn Days

'September blow soft, Till the fruits are in the loft,' or 'September dries up wells and breaks down bridges.'

So, a new month, a colourful month of leaves turning and of wild fruit ripening up for the wild creatures to eat, and for our apple and blackberry pies.

I saw a water shrew sunning itself on a flat stone by a stream just the other day. It is a quiet backwater of a place and water shrews have been about there for as long as I can recall. Very dark coats they have, velvety black with white beneath, the demarcation line clearly showing. And water shrews sing beautifully.

With a small territory, water shrews are easy to observe and, as their eyesight is adapted to their lifestyle, they do not see us if we keep still.

Their movement is like the water itself: they seem to trickle and dart about as to the currents and eddies below the weir. Then, into the water from another stone at the stream edge, the little mammal turning silver with the air bubbles trapped in its soft coat. Almost fish-like for a moment until the little legs get working; the tail acts as a sort of rudder. A miniature otter in a way, about three inches long with a tail to match.

Water shrews, then, are rather larger than the other shrews, and a treat to watch, waterways being fine places for wildlife observation. Follow the usual rule, though. Find a good spot and settle down to observe. Footfalls, vibrations, movement, and shadows cast on the water do little to help the observer who wants to watch a wild creature properly. Fleeting glimpses are the alternative for the nature-watcher on the move. One does not learn much that away, even though country walking is a lovely thing to do.

With heart-jolting suddenness I saw the stag in the shadow of the trees. Another twenty paces and I would have had the greater shock of walking into him – not that he would have allowed that to happen.

Bracken the collie was way up the slope, having detoured to avoid cattle in the field. The stag was wearing a full head of antlers. Magnificent is the word. He grunted a half-roar and shook his head. Bracken stopped and was gazing down our way, his pricked ears like a black butterfly. I looked back at the stag which was already walking into the woods without a sound. He was in view again for half a minute as he broke cover in the evening sunshine to cross a stubble field and then I lost him.

High in the tree canopy three pied flycatchers sought out insects. Probably the ones that nested here in the boxes, two males and a female. They will soon be on their way to northern Iberia, probably Portugal. Here flycatchers set up defended territories for a while as they put on weight for further flight to tropical West Africa.

I shall miss the summer birds and the summer. Autumn and winter are very beautiful and full of interest, but I am fond of birdsong and summer warmth. However, there is plenty to come before winter sets in, and a fair period of Indian summer, too, which will shorten the winter.

A question-mark still hangs over why flycatchers do not inhabit south-eastern England, but I think it is because they require woodlands with sparse shrub layers.

That autumn chill has been about in the mornings for a while now. On go the jumpers to keep us warm, in line with the wild creatures putting on thicker coats.

We were watching two little grebes, or dabchicks, fishing in a tributary of the main river here, diving with scarcely a ripple in the wide pool formed by a meander of the waterway. They bred this year on the nearby marshes.

Little grebes are the smallest of their family and the most widespread. I have watched them in the highlands of Scotland and on tiny ponds in Cornwall, their love of still and slow-moving water and plenty of cover being the main criteria attracting them, along with food, of course. If they are going for a deep dive, they will make a little jump and a tiny splash as they enter the water. You will know from this that they will be down longer and are probably fishing deeply. They take insects, and always seem busy.

This pair were still in their summer plumage with the red necks and small white patch at the base of the bill clearly showing. Later they will become dull brown above and buff and white below, the winter plumage of the species being much less colourful than their summer plumage.

Do remember the often striking differences in seasonal plumage in birds if you are just starting bird-watching. At this time of year especially, and in the spring, the changing colour patterns may have you searching the books in puzzled manner.

One of the lovelier sights of nature is that of little grebes swimming across a reedy pond with newly hatched youngsters on their backs. But we will have to wait until next year to see that.

Drizzly rain in the valley but along the middle path it was barely noticeable. One of the many favourite spots in Sanctuary Wood is a miniature 'cave' that goes back into the underground root system of an oak tree. Being on a steep slope, the gnarled roots have become exposed over the years on the downward side of the tree and little caverns have formed. The cave is lit with a green glow, shining quite ethereally. I always pause at this spot to enjoy the beautiful sight – the emerald mine, as Robin calls it.

I think what makes the glow is the moss *Schistostega pennata*. But, as it seems not to have an English name, I am naming it 'emerald glow', for Robin, and not straining my brain trying to recall its other name.

It is colourful now along the wood edge and within, among the trees. There are plenty of rose-hips and haws about, plus a lot of wild arum, otherwise known as lords and ladies, in scarlet array.

Rose-hips are well known for being rich in vitamin C. You can make a sweet drink quite easily by boiling the berries into a syrup, to take advantage of the build-up of vitamin C before the winter. It is like drinking sunshine.

Some creatures have already laid down winter supplies well in advance. Just as last year, we have found an old nest, a robin's this time, stocked up with the fruits of alder, buckthorn and the wild rose-hips, with a few blackberries. This will be the store of a woodmouse. We found another too, a tiny heap of fruits hidden under the roots.

After a night and day of rain the evening became still and pleasantly fine. We went out with Bracken to enjoy the river view and the fresh air.

Bracken submerged his nose and head to find the largest stone in the stream, while we savoured some of the last remnants of summer. The weir was black polished water beneath the trees, thrusting down into the white, foaming weir-splash then on to the main stream, sparkling and noisy with life sounds.

Sometimes the roar of water is a blessing. This evening a kingfisher perched on the old sluice machinery, its chestnut breast brighter than the rusty iron which it gripped with sealing-wax red feet. We were able to watch the kingfisher for a dozen minutes before it flew downstream to the spinney which hangs over the water.

The stream was deeper here than it had been for weeks, but if the rain keeps off the water can drop a foot in height in a day. In a stormy week it will go up and down like a yo-yo.

There is a fine guelder-rose tree growing just by the weir. In the old days they called it by the better name of swamp elder, which pointed to the tree's liking for the wet and the elder-like berries which are forming now as the leaves colour up.

The true elder is common along the mill leat here, growing well with alder. It is without doubt one of the finest medicinal trees and popular with real gypsies for that reason. We used to make very good whistles from elder as the pithy centre of the twigs and branches was easy enough for a schoolboy to hollow out. A few holes notched down one side and you had a free penny whistle.

Blackberry picking along Marsh field is always pleasant. I still find it incredible that there are some four hundred different types of bramble in Britain.

But they do differ, and quite markedly. In just a few yards of hedgerow there are large, juicy fruits along with tighter, much harder kinds, with widely varying flavours.

It was beautiful there, miles from town noises. We had swished through tall grass and water mint; the scent of the mint was strong on the air. Honeysuckle displayed all its variety in the one great mass that hung amongst the alder and hawthorn. Swathes of flowers in creams through to purple-red, buds waiting to bloom, and both green and red berries on show. Thankfully, it had been raining, and the scent of honeysuckle was up and mingling with the water mint perfume.

On the latter's lilac blooms were two painted lady butterflies, migrants that seem to get everywhere when they do arrive. One of these had bluish spots on the hind wings, circled by black, and very darkly marked edges to the wings, while some of the forewing markings were cream instead of white. This specimen possibly had a hint of melanism, the pigmentation that causes dark colour forms in many creatures. An aberration to be photographed and noted carefully in the notebook.

Unless you are carrying a camera to record finds, a notebook and sketches recording as much detail as possible, plus the date, time, weather conditions, and even the plant the creature is on, are invaluable for later reference. Relying on one's memory never works as well as careful note-making.

We have been keeping an eye on a location where a female otter has been moving with two cubs. There is one spot on the waterway where it is possible to see along to the holt where the cubs were born. A hundred yards of water shimmering in greens and browns until the evening sunset lights it green and gold.

If we are lucky a wide V-shaped wake shows where the bitch otter is moving out to see all is well. On three occasions we have seen the two cubs follow her out, but most times footprints in the mud are the signs that tell us they are still there.

This evening all three swam about near the holt for half an hour, occasionally climbing out onto the bank, then into the water again, not even fishing, just enjoying the place. They will fish later, when the moon is up.

The cubs are about five or six months old. Around January or February they will disperse, a cold time to become independent, but otters may be born at any time of the year.

A red sympetrum dragonfly flew to perch on the bankside vegetation to roost for the night. Even as we watched, the glinting wings lost their shine. The sun was dipping away. It was time to go. Creaking upright we moved off along the darkening lane, where lights switching on at the old millhouse made it seem all the darker.

The smell of fresh baked bread wafted from an open window. There is a comfort in such a scent, but not in eating hot bread. Country folk will tell you, eat fresh bread, yes, but not hot bread, nor old or stale bread, for it dries up the natural moisture in the body.

❖ ❦ ❖

The gentle pattering of bird droppings onto my companion's shoulder brought with it a little natural history lesson.

'See, the bird has been eating blackberries and elderberries,' I said, the lurid purple colouring being the evidence.

'I'd rather observe a paper tissue right now,' he said.

We'd seen blackbirds and starlings eating berries that morning and had found badger droppings in a latrine constructed just below and away from an ancient sett. It also contained plum stones from some nearby orchard or garden.

My companion, a fastidious sort of chap, was none too interested in such observations. I was about to tell him it was said to bring good luck having a bird announce its presence in this way, when he slipped and found one of the few cowpats for yards around.

We decided to return home and on the way, at the bottom of an oak I was able to point out a nuthatch pushing a hazelnut into a crevice in the bark. Five nuts it stored in this manner, eating none, though often these birds will use the bark as a vice to hold the nut while they smash the shell open for the fruit – hence 'nut-hatchet', the origin of their name.

My companion had never seen this behaviour before and was delighted to add a new sighting to his notebook. We watched the little masked bird for a while, then went on our way.

Reading through an old country book dated 1864 I came across a chapter on making nestbox provision for barn owls in order to encourage them to stay on your land to keep down vermin. Certainly, we cannot assume that looking after such birds with nestboxes is a new idea, though the barn owl would have been commoner then than now.

There are a few near our home. One pair regularly winter-roost near by but cross the river to breed through the spring and summer.

I was told recently of one that flies into a house to roost on a sideboard each day, then goes out hunting by night. The house is occupied and fully furnished. Lovely that, a dream of a situation.

Years ago I saw a tawny owl taking fish from a mill leat, deliberately hunting in this manner and being very successful at it. Recently, a farmer's wife told me how a barn owl was catching fish in the large fishpond on her farm using the same method as an osprey, dropping straight down on them from the air.

Her husband described how, when his father farmed the land, a fox used to fish from the weir pool and how the owls would create havoc among the haystooks, rats and mice running all ways when the birds were hunting. He told me his father built a tree-house on a platform for him and his brother, and tawny owls took it over as their nest site for three consecutive years.

In my experience tawny owls will take as readily to buildings as barn owls, commonly roosting in empty or derelict houses, usually on windowsills with a good view over surrounding countryside, or in barn lofts, in identical situations to those favoured by their pale, white cousins.

October is a good time for hunting fungi with sketchbook and pencil or camera. Sketchpads with all-weather paper (especially good in misty or rainy conditions) and water-soluble coloured pencils are excellent for this purpose, allowing for dry and watercolour pictures to be made on the spot.

If one keeps a good point on the pencils they produce really fine detail.

Growing from the short turf of the clifftops we saw parasol fungi, never better described than by Henry Williamson, who likened their subtle buff and darker brown markings to the plumage of a barn owl. A perfect description. At this time of year they grow profusely in many a Westcountry site.

If there are artists' fungi, I suppose fly agaric with its red cap and white speckles would be the most painted, perhaps along with the huge dryads' saddles, a type of bracket fungi which grows from the trunks of frees.

The poisonous fly agaric is very well known, yet probably few have seen it in the wild. It presents a striking picture, usually growing in association with birch trees or conifers. The cap is surrounded by veils which tear as it enlarges. It is the fragments of the universal veil which remain attached to the red cap that give the white-patch effect.

The double-note call of the stock dove, 'coo-coo', came from the stand of old trees at the edge of Brock Cleave. Here in open countryside with old trees the species is at its happiest, as are wood pigeons of course. They are similar in appearance although the stock dove bears more resemblance to the town pigeon. When it is perched it is easy to see that the white neck-patches, which are so conspicuous in the wood pigeon, are missing.

Stock doves nest in tree holes more often than not, but I have found them nesting in old rabbit burrows in a wood and once in a nestbox placed for owls. Recently we saw a pair at a rock crevice on the coast and they do frequent coastal as well as inland habitats.

As with other pigeons, the young, called squabs, feed on pigeon's milk from the adult's throat for a while before taking greenstuff. They may be born any time between March and October.

When they are in flight look for two short, black-looking bars on each wing; wood pigeons have white wing patches. Generally speaking, they are smaller, stockier birds than other pigeons and do not have the white rumps of rock doves so there should be no difficulty in identification.

There should be more wood pigeons about now, coming to our shores and building up the numbers of birds wintering here. Already the starling flocks are foraging about the countryside. Their numbers rise sharply at this time of year as they fly in from Europe and colder climes.

I love the sound of the pigeons in the woodlands, a lovely, almost lazy, relaxing sound, rather comforting as you walk the countryside.

It was an overcast, still morning, even the autumn colours seemed subdued, yet it was a morning brightened by the cheery song of robins. By tradition, today (22 October) is one of the great commemoration days in nature, the greatest, we might say, for as James Usher noted in *The Annals of the World* in 1658, according to ancient chronology it is the anniversary of the Creation.

There were woodcock in the woods. Three put up from the narrow path, for it was early yet and we were the first to disturb them. The birds flew low and headed out of the trees and across the river to the valley on the other side, more amenable country for them, away from human pressures. Migrants these, building up their numbers. I shall look forward to seeing them during the winter.

Once it was thought that woodcock arrived here from the moon. John Gay wrote in 1714: 'Some think to the northern coasts their flight they tend, Or to the moon in midnight hours ascend.' He had it half right, which is pretty good for 280 years ago.

A glint of pinkish-red showed in the sky over Exmoor way, the early morning sun breaking through the cloud cover but warning of rain at the same time. By the time we had reached the river it was showing as a glowing orange orb. A heron put up from the tide-pool on the saltings with a screeching cry. Maybe this is how primeval Creation looked and sounded, wild and beautiful.

Sloe time. I see there are some nice sloes about still for those partial to the taste. The blossoms and juice of sloes have been used in country medicines for many years, and the leaves of the tree make a tea.

The blackthorn is also one of the two ancestors of all the cultivated plums we now enjoy, so when we see its fruit in the hedgerows we should respect it for itself and for all that it has given us over the years. And a blackthorn walking stick is one of the finest. I miss my old one, which did twenty years' walking with me.

Some years ago a retired farmer told me he had a 'crystal' tree in his garden and I should come and see it. He assured me it was a Devon name though I did not know it. Intrigued, I went along and there learned of the old cultivated plum, the bullace, long abandoned for more popular varieties but a lovely old tree to be introduced to.

There were three in the hedge of what was an old orchard, the farmer making bullace or 'crystal' wine from the fruit which he said was as good as any port. There are just two left there now, and a stump remaining of the third.

Doing some homework, I found the fruit was also known as keslings and that the tree itself was known as wild damson in some parts. In Somerset they called the fruit Christians.

Fascinating, these country names. Christians, crystals – the two must be from the same source. Some more homework may discover what it is.

❖ ❦ ❖

Acorns 'rained' in the woodland. They seem to choose the same moment to fall, making muffled thuds as they hit grass and pathway. Deer like them, competing with jays, pigeons, squirrels and woodmice for the goodness in the oak-fruit. Cattle have overeaten on them and suffered from acorn poisoning.

Below the top path the bracken is an untidy, beautiful bronze mass. I shall leave it until February, then cut it on a dry day and stack it against the bank at the wood edge to rot down. Through the winter it will be shelter for any creature needing a blanket of bracken as extra cover over its lair.

Here the fern also blankets the bluebells. Its removal in February or March is followed in April and May by a bluebell carpet. When they are over the fresh green of new bracken bursts through.

But I'm jumping the gun, let's enjoy the current season.

Among the bracken are some puffball fungi. A gentle tap releases thousands of spores, just a few of which will find exactly the right conditions for germination. This is why so many spores are produced in the first place, millions to ensure the survival of a few. It has been calculated that one ripe field mushroom can produce 1000 million spores at a rate of 40 million per hour! Astonishing.

It was getting late so I decided not to check these figures; more sense to pick a few fungi and contemplate such matters while eating them.

How quickly night falls now, and far too early. It falls like a plummeting acorn. With the acorns and the autumn leaf-fall came a heavy mist sweeping across the valley. Time to go home.

❖ ❦ ❖

What does tameness or wildness really, mean I wonder? Yesterday I rested paper, with a couple of sandwiches in it, upon a flat stone wall as I ate and sat watching the view and Bracken nosing about near by.

A long-tailed field mouse appeared on the wall beside me and with slow jerky movements and much twitching of nose and whiskers gradually made its way to the sandwiches. I waylaid it by breaking off some bread and cheese and holding it just in front of the creature, whom I expected to run off. Not a bit of it.

The mouse sniffed, then nibbled, attacking the cheese and then the bread with gusto. She sat up and cleaned her face as I broke off a larger portion. There was no sign of fear; food had won me a friend.

She promptly waded into the second helping and then a third, by which time I could stroke her sun-warmed back. Still chewing, she permitted this for a while and then waddled plumply along the wall and into a crevice in the stonework. I peered in, to see her tucked up on dried grass and already fast asleep.

I now know that long-tailed field mice like a strong-tasting Cheddar.

I am no longer surprised by the behaviour of wildlife, no matter how unusual it may appear. Delighted, yes; surprised, no. More and more one comes to realise what a fine borderline there is twixt fear and friendship as far as animals and man are concerned. The rapport is often remarkable; there must be a sensing between the two that all is well. Maybe it's an aura thing.

Whatever the reason, I shall cherish the experience and hope it will occur again, a little mouse making a day special.

Wintertime

Exmoor in winter is marred only by the shortness of the days. For some reason winter seems longer than summer but knowing this we can make allowances.

Gallivanting over the moors on a November day, every minute is worthwhile. If we choose the coast of Exmoor, with a view where the sun sets over the sea, we can at least prolong the day a little.

If you have not visited Exmoor and its coastline, try to picture a Scotland in miniature. (If you have not visited Scotland either, do try one or the other if time permits.)

Much of the coast is a series of wonderful hog's-back cliffs, the landscape undulating like the flight of a green woodpecker and just as green for much of it is clothed in hanging woodlands. Occasionally a valley will break the coast.

The Vale of Porlock, both beautiful and interesting, is one such. Much of the former seabed grows arable crops, while saltmarshes and a broad sweep of shingle vary the view. There is excellent birding to be had in this area amidst a green agricultural belt that sees good weather for much of the time, good to the extent that Porlockers often have to mow their lawns all year round. Porlock used to be a port but it seems to have moved inland with the passing of time and the changes in human activity.

The saltmarshes, reedbeds, lakes and old pastures provide a richness and diversity for the nature-watcher that makes this part of Exmoor's beautiful coastline very different. The Westcountry is a good place to live and the quieter places are all the better for being out on a limb.

Thanks largely to its altitude and climate Dartmoor survives as an unspoilt granite landscape with areas of wilderness. Its natural beauty acts as a magnet to all those who love to commune with Nature. No doubt becoming a National Park has helped to ensure that it remains a wilderness, but somehow I feel that would have been the way of it in any case. Dartmoor is Dartmoor, its very being resistant to much change.

Agriculture here is difficult and rainfall heavy. At Princetown, for example, it is 85 inches a year. That's wetter than one can get in the Plume of Feathers in the village!

They say that the dangers of the bogs on Westcountry moors are exaggerated in books like Conan Doyle's *Hound of the Baskervilles*, set here on Dartmoor, or Blackmore's *Lorna Doone*, set on Exmoor. Well, get on to either moor during rainy, misty times, on your own or with a friend, and see how you feel when the landscape vanishes and your boots are sucked off. In those writers' days a tarmac road and cosy car were not part of the scene, either.

I've sat with a ring ouzel at Fox Tor and a dotterel on Dunkery when the mists have fallen fast and if they didn't know what to do, or where to go, I certainly didn't. Blanketing mists can fall very swiftly, within seconds even, but they can stay for hours on end. So if you are nature-watching in the wilds at this time of year, be sure someone knows where you are going.

❄ ❄ ❄

A still morning but a watery light and grey clouds heavy with rain suggested we move fast to avoid the threatened downpour.

On a sort of shelf at eye-level were Pixie-cup lichens, a most beautiful winter lichen and exactly as the name suggests, tiny cups asking to be used by Little People.

Moorhens were having an argument somewhere along the ditch, their calls loud and fierce, but try as I might I could not see them, just some old thistles waving and jostling about. If one locked long enough at the plants in the greenish half-light of the ditch tunnel it was easy to imagine it was they who were arguing, the sound coming from that spot.

I watched and listened for a while and then all was quiet. Two moorhens moved out onto the pooled water and went their separate ways in peace, trails of dark water cutting through the green blanket of duckweed as they went.

A robin sang from the twists of hawthorn roots by the waterside. I remembered Longfellow's verse about Mother Nature, the old Nurse:

And whenever the way seemed long,
Or his heart began to fail,
She would sing a more wonderful song,
Or tell a more marvellous tale.

Longfellow understood the balance of nature. This may be a term recently coined to help us grasp the complex system of links between all creatures and plants, but it can also mean something deeper and very relevant to modern humans. When the hassles of the everyday take over one's thoughts and the clock, Mother Nature is there to provide the balance and the lift we all need at times.

❄ ❄ ❄

Like a whirlwind, the flock of starlings, thousands strong, spiralled and spread and closed ranks again as the birds swept in a mass across the hillside. It is always a splendid sight, awesome if one is close beneath, for the sound of rushing wings is loud, the sky blackened.

We had gone specially to watch the spectacle, having been tipped off about the starlings' nightly coming-to-roost.

On they came, sweeping down towards a stand of trees, a snaking cloud of birds, and out of the lone oak standing some fifty yards from the roost clump came a sparrowhawk. Straight into the oncoming mass she flew, penetrating deeply, then a flapping of wings and she was out of the mêlée with a bird in her grasp. A case of the multitude feeding the one.

The picture before us was now one of hawk and prey in the lone oak and settling starlings disappearing into the still leafy branches of the others, noisy now as starlings are at roost, squawking and chattering, but giving no sign of tension although a predator was about. Most of them may have been unaware that the hawk had been and gone, the tail end of the huge flock being many yards back from the leaders.

This was in all likelihood a nightly occurrence, with the possibility that the hawk breakfasted here as well. A brave sparrowhawk to fly into that lot – and unusual not to see the flock divide and swirl about the raptor as I have witnessed before.

These roosts are like magnets. Sparrowhawks, owls, even peregrines will attack them, as will mink from the ground. With roosts numbering tens of thousands, millions even, the losses to predators in terms of overall population are minute.

❄ ❄ ❄

A smouldering bonfire in the farmyard sent a plume of blue smoke up to hedge-top height then along towards the spinney as the wind caught it, a pleasant smell of woodsmoke and the scene peaceful with rows of planted kale and deep puddles reflecting the rain clouds that had left them along the lane. Gnats danced in swarms. They always seem to be swirling at great speed but if you single out individuals you realise it is not so, the swirling numbers producing an optical illusion of speed.

Lapwings passed overhead, silvery-white and black with broad wings beating slow and mothlike. Lapwings will often feed in the farmfields, especially if the estuary tide is in. No sign of the green of the plovers' plumage today.

There was a lot of chattering and twittering along the hedge – the redwings were moving across country seeking out berries to eat. Already the haws are mostly gone and the thrushes are finding it hard to sate their hunger. No doubt the redwings have helped deplete the hedgerow fruits for they have been here from the North quite a while now. I saw my first flock of the year on 21 October and this species, along with fieldfares, makes short work of available food.

Both species may breed in the far north of Scotland. I well recall thinking we had found a nesting song thrush in Inverness one year, only to discover that a pair of redwings had chosen a spot near a white-water river island overlooking a common sandpiper's nest on the shingly island itself. Most of our wintering redwings and fieldfares arrive from Scandinavian countries.

A cold, wet afternoon, darkness coming on early and the wind suggesting icy weather up ahead with the likelihood of a freeze-up.

Much of our landscape was shaped in the Ice Ages, when great sheets of ice spread from Scandinavian mountains to cover the British Isles, reaching to the Severn, the Thames and beyond. Huge rocks were brought to England from Norway. The Severn flowed into the Irish Sea until ice shifted its flow into the Bristol Channel.

There are rock 'erratics' on Westcountry beaches including red sandstone from Scotland, now here in Devon thanks to Ice Age movement. Many natural lakes are said to have been scooped out by ice, some reaching below sea-level. We visited Loch Morar in Inverness-shire, said to be 1017 feet deep.

Many of our mountain ridges' deepest U-shaped valleys and river directions were ice-formed. Indeed parts of East Anglia would be below sea level had not the ice deposited layers of boulder clay and gravel up to 100 feet in depth.

Ice action on rock is devastating stuff, best witnessed today perhaps in the many scree slopes in valleys and coombes. These are the rocky piles on sloping hillsides, also called talus, the slopes constantly a little over 30 degrees.

Few plants gain a roothold on scree slopes where the fragments are coarse, but it makes an interesting study to spend time observing such an area near one's home, particularly to spot shifts and new colonisers over the course of a few years. Lichens are usually the first colonisers and here in the wetter West with relatively unpolluted air this dual plant, formed by a fungus and a plant of the algae group, can thrive.

❄ ❄ ❄

We found winter cress along a stream bank recently, just on one side, for quite a stretch. The stream is one I have not explored that often so I shall be back next summer to photograph the yellow blooms, which look like wall-flowers.

Winter cress was used as a salad and highly valued for its culinary uses but more modern vegetables appeared and it lost its popularity. Readers may know the double-flowered variety grown in gardens, called yellow rocket. Once the plant was called wound rocket (a name which never took off) because, like yarrow, it was good for treating wounds. In Cornwall it was casabully and land cress, and in Somerset St Barbara's herb.

In fact it was a plant given to St Barbara in many European countries and is properly named *Barbarea vulgaris.* As her festival is 4 December, maybe that is the reason for the link, for it is green throughout the winter.

There was a water rail along the stream, nice and secluded here; it is a species that prefers to hide from mankind.

Then a snipe put up from under my feet, flying silently away for a short distance to resume feeding. It was the silence that had me looking more closely and the fact that it flew straight and dropped quickly back to cover. Binoculars showed it to be as I'd hoped, a Jack Snipe, the double pale streaks across its crown and the shorter-looking bill all helping identify the species. It may have been hereabouts for a while. I put it up once more to be sure and there was no doubt of its identity. A lovely little snipe. Jack is a word our ancestors used to mean small or undersized.

❄ ❄ ❄

It is river-eel fishing time, once very popular in the countryside. Clatting for eels was a favourite pastime and these days they fetch a pretty price. One old way was to make a sort of bottle or tube of hay wrapped round with willow boughs and filled with offal. This was submerged in deep water by the river-bank and after two or three days the eels would be in and caught.

An elderly gentleman I knew who taught me a lot used to go clatting for eels with a great ball of wool fashioned in much the same way. He made a dugout canoe from a Thuya pine trunk some years ago and would fish the rivers in it with his terrier dog sitting in the bows. He fashioned the canoe from the Thuya with a sharp axe.

I saw a similar dugout in Scotland cut from a Scots pine. The owner, whose grandfather had passed it down to him, told me that the canoe-maker would use fire to help fashion the craft. The log would be kept moist while this process was carried out, thus producing a sort of plasticity that greatly aided the making and waterproofing of the canoe.

Dugouts are probably the oldest form of navigable craft, along with coracles, and were the best mode of transport for Native Americans who roved the rivers and lakes in them.

Thuya pines were once popular as ornamentals, and these western red cedars were also planted in forests for their timber, which is durable and light in weight. One sees them singly along green lanes on occasion, planted I suspect when these routes were part of large estates, as so many country lanes and trackways once were.

❄ ❄ ❄

It had rained all day with no sign of a let-up and darkness was not far away. It was time to give Bracken a long run.

Beech leaves strewn by autumn along the lane were aglow with rainshine and quite a few branches were down and broken across the path. Do trees kindly drop branches in the early hours to avoid hurting people? Rarely have I seen them fall yet there were several on the route to the river. Alder and hazel catkins are showing, the former's purple colour enhanced by the wetness and the raindrops hanging from each.

The rain came down harder. Numerous beetles and chiggy-pigs were swept out onto the wood path. Although the chiggy-pigs (or woodlice) like damp, this was somewhat moister than they would wish. How quickly they regain their feet.

Bracken looked at me dolefully. The surface water run-off was incredible. I felt as if Grace Darling would be along in a boat at any minute! We turned back and Bracken, his tail up, trotted homeward, preferring this direction under the sheltering oaks.

Grace Darling's epic rescue of a shipwrecked crew is commemorated by the planting of several oaks, including a turkey oak in Battersea Park, London. The wonderfully brave woman died only four years after the event, of tuberculosis, but she will be remembered in the trees planted for her.

It is a good time to plant a tree now. I understand Devon County Council have no 'free tree' scheme this year, but buying and planting a tree must be one of the best ways to spend a few pounds.

❄ ❄ ❄

For a good walk on Dartmoor, or even a few shorter walks, try the Mariners' Way which winds along the eastern side of the moor. Running from the port of Bideford to the port of Dartmouth, this route was the sailors' way over this delightful moorland and it is said that there used to be rest-houses every ten or so miles.

Part of the route is from South Zeal to Widecombe, through interesting countryside for the nature-lover. I did a ten- or eleven-mile walk from Clannaborough to a place called Natsworthy, a ways up from Widecombe church. I could have done with an old grey mare along the paths that link the two sites. The Ordnance Survey Pathfinder map series is really excellent for this type of walking but anyone contemplating much wildlife walking is better with the 2½-inch sheets.

I liked Heathercombe, and the various little bridges, ash houses, farm buildings, standing stones and birdlife. Unusually for one daylight ramble, we saw six foxes. They stopped to take a gander at us just as we did at them; quite bold and curious they were.

I find moorland foxes quite different from low-country foxes in that they pay far less heed to the presence of mankind. Less harassment, probably.

The coombes were deep in mist, the high ground like giant's stepping-stones to some mysterious lost world, but no black hounds here; just the foxes in their rust-coloured beauty, appearing and disappearing into the cloud-filled coombes as if to say 'Follow me.'

But we didn't. Instead we played it safe, watching a flock of golden plovers pass over quite low, and some dark geese, a hundred or more, much higher and difficult to identify with any certainty.

❄ ❄ ❄

It was a good bit of ploughing, the field neatly turned and half-hidden in the morning mist. Standing in the open gateway, I jumped as a flock of redwings and fieldfares came at me out of the mist. They swarmed up as they shirred overhead and down the hillside.

A badger followed them, walking of course, not flying. The old term 'pake' describes well his aimless saunter. The badger was a large boar, no doubt homeward bound from foraging. I heard him grunt and snuffle his way into a gorse brake and he was gone.

The gorse had quite a lot of golden flowers upon it, rather spring-like and uplifting to see. There is a lot of it visible from the cleave slope, enjoying respite after many years of providing fodder for cattle. Now it's a nursery for badger and fox cubs.

Two kinds of gorse grow commonly in the Westcountry: common gorse and western gorse, the latter a low-growing shrub often found on the coast. Gorse is a member of the pea family. It is known as whin in Scotland, hence whinchat for the summer-visiting bird rather similar to a stonechat. Whin bark is still used today to make a traditional yellow dye for tartan cloth. Lovely that the old dyeing methods are still used, producing some wonderful colours in subtle country shades.

❄ ❄ ❄

A friend living in London writes to say how boring Christmas becomes when all the stores there have been flogging it to death since September. Of course Christmas, supposedly celebrated for the birth of Christ, is big business and less commonly a spiritual event. However, it does seem to revive in most a more brotherly or sisterly attitude for a while. That is pleasant in itself, though it would be better if it could be maintained all year round.

There are some interesting nature lore aspects to Christmas. The ash tree is renowned as the farmer's tree because its wood, used for fences, tool handles, and in carts and wagons, is a lovely close-grained wood, smooth to the touch. Ash is also the proper wood for a shepherd's crook, for it was believed that ash would never injure livestock. But in Ireland and parts of the Westcountry ash faggots were burned to banish the devil, particularly at Christmas-time and especially in Devon, where the practice remains in some areas. It is said that Christ's mother Mary washed and dressed Him for the very first time in front of an ash-wood fire.

We all know how closely holly is linked with Christmas. When I was a lad the cut branches of holly were actually named 'Christmas' and we were thus gathering Christmas from the hedgerows. On the tree, each leaf of the holly lasts for up to four years, but if frost locks up supplies of water the younger leaves fall off. The same applies during droughts. The bright red berries are of course an important food supply for several bird species, including blackbirds and thrushes.

❄ ❄ ❄

On the coast path, against a dry stone wall which with the gorse bushes sheltered us from an onshore wind, was the sloughed skin of an adder. It was held fast by a stone and must have lain for many weeks while scores of walkers passed it by. Adders are hibernating now and we would not see any about until the spring.

I found an adder's skull not far from here a few years ago, intact with the wonderful array of teeth pointing sharply back down the throat. So light and fragile was it that when I rested it on the wall to find a plastic bag, a gust of wind blew it away and I never found it again.

Adders are not aggressive towards man though they will quite rightly defend themselves if they feel threatened. A bit of respect and caution is all that is required; that is to say, leave them well alone.

On the rocks far below the path a peregrine was eating a pigeon. In the glasses every movement showed clear. The raptor would not go hungry today. Several jackdaws in a flock dipped to see what the falcon was about, then chattered on to some cliff hideout; they are common on the coast here.

A fallen tree lay near a stile and climbing over we dislodged some rotten timber which in turn dislodged a few beetles. Amongst them to my delight and surprise were several ladybirds, including two of the bright green variety of the ten-spot ladybird. Its edges were studded black and gold, the green a true apple green.

What prizes here, hidden away on a winter's day, tiny and quite uncommon, buried treasure revealed by accident: serendipity – that lovely term – at work as ever.

Endymion went searching to see which wild flowers were still in bloom and found hogweed, daisy, dandelion, hawkbit, hedge woundwort, scentless mayweed, groundsel, wild carrot, wild strawberry, nettles, campion and herb robert, bindweed and yellow archangel; it was like a summer's day in winter. Naturally the flowers were few and far between, but hedge woundwort! Such an interesting way to spend an hour, with notes in the diary to compare with other years as well as entertaining oneself during a walk in the rain.

If you are carrying binoculars, reverse them and look into the object lens at plants and other things you want to see in close-up. They make an excellent portable microscope.

Walking homeward along a farm track, we spotted chickens in a wired enclosure in a paddock. Plenty of room here, a free-ranging chicken run. These were the popular Rhode Island reds, probably the chickens I knew best as a lad, when free range was the only way and hens quite commonly laid eggs under the hedges.

Keeping chickens was very popular in the 1940s. The Rhode Island red is said to have been developed in the 1880s in New England, in the United States, with a mixed ancestry of local breeds and birds from Asia. On a farm near my boyhood home I also remember the Light Sussex and the Buff Orpington, which also seems to have had a mixed ancestry. I wonder whether, with the demand for free-range eggs, we will see the attractive old breeds about the countryside again.

You rarely hear the cockerel crowing these days. A wonderful country sound, sadly missed, like elm trees, scribbles from chip shops, and bags of broken biscuits.

A song thrush feeds her young in the peaceful seclusion of a nest sheltered by ivy. The species was once far more common, but there are signs of a reversal of its decline.

A male orange tip butterfly basks in the nectar-providing sanctuary of a Westcountry garden habitat. Jack-by-the-hedge and lady's smock are sought-after food plants.

The beautiful berries of the wild guelder rose tree brightening a chilly autumn day.

A male banded demoiselle damselfly perches in a summer reedbed. A species sensitive to pollution it needs healthy emergent plants for egg-laying.

Razorbills, like guillemots and puffins, are members of the auk family. Very much a breeding bird of the Westcountry's rugged, rocky coastline.

Wild arum berries – 'snakefood' in country folklore, to remind us that the berries are poisonous to humans – were once (erroneously) thought to provide adders with their venom. The berries are the fruit of parson-in-the-pulpit and lords and ladies, old country names of the plant.

Autumn splendour. Tawny grisettes are both beautiful and edible fungi, often associated with birch trees.

Badgers at a sett entrance in a wooded valley. The are clean animals which regularly change their bedding and dig lairines away from the sett.

A group of red deer hinds and their calves at a favourite Exmoor drinking place.

Like dark arrows the starlings zoom everywhere, their numbers greatly increased by winter migrants. The air temperatures have changed so slowly this year, with the remarkably mild November seeing swallows that should have long gone. The appearance of two starlings carrying twigs and a blackbird carrying moss was quite a surprise, however. I doubt if they will breed; surely a touch of cold will soon arrive.

Along the top path a field mushroom stood large, growing white and shining from leaf mulch, beside fruiting wild strawberries which remain yellow and unripe. The mushroom had bites taken from around its edge. Closer examination showed squirrel pawmarks deeply indented where the animal had held the cap fast while eating.

Tracks and signs. They take us closer to the nature of things. We can all be budding Sherlocks and it is a good interest for youngsters. There is no suffering from boredom if one takes an interest in natural history. A good way to start a youngster off is to instil the sense of questioning and wonderment.

Probably the best-known track of all is that of the snail wandering across a garden path. It is a doorway to exploration, for it leads one to wonder from where it comes, and to where it goes, and to learn of the creature's ways.

From snail tracks to leaf-miner beetles, to muddy places with animal and bird track marks, is a fascinating way to develop skills of observation that will have us wanting to get out and about. A hand lens, then, and a book on tracks and signs, for good Christmas explorations.

❄ ❄ ❄

Wells is a lovely place to visit with much for the naturalist to enjoy, including the sculptures in the cathedral. These include birds preening, an animal licking its coat clean, a fox with a goose and birds with human heads. There is a bird with a frog in its bill and, for those interested in cryptozoology, a human-like creature with a fish's tail, holding a fish. Carved figures of apple-pickers and people with toothache or thorns in the foot suggest a closeness to the reality of nature and the countryside which makes the awe-inspiring building so much more homely and friendly.

Closeness to nature is part and parcel of Wells, with nearby Wookey Hole and the Great Cave once inhabited by Celts, by hyenas and by the witch of Wookey. The River Axe flows here and in and out of the Wookey Hole caves into lovely bird-watching countryside. Cheddar and Axbridge are just north-west of here along a seaward line under the Mendip Hills to Weston Bay.

Close by is one of the Westcountry's most fascinating National Nature Reserves, the landslip area which extends five miles from the mouth of the Axe eastward to Lyme Regis. Is another great landslip waiting to happen here? Likely it is. The one on Christmas Eve 1839 was the most impressive of modern slips.

Here lie ichthyosaurs, molluscs, ammonites, and much else. We found rockrose, fen orchid, bog pimpernel, carline thistle, buzzards and sparrowhawks, woodpeckers, whitethroats, nightingales and rock pipits here on a summer's day. A rich mix of wildlife.

❄ ❄ ❄

For the third time in many years of nightwatching for wildlife I have witnessed an incident that seems to transcend others and leaves me deeply moved. We had been quietly watching three or four badgers on the cleave slope for about three-quarters of an hour when they all turned to face the sett, standing stock still. Another badger moved onto the hillside, a bit odd-looking until we realised it was being pushed from the sett entrance by another. The first badger was dead. Its mate – I guessed it was its mate – nudged it onto the slope until it rolled down for some thirty to forty yards to rest against the bramble brake there.

It was difficult to tell boar from sow in the shadows of the moonlit field but the bereaved badger was a female, I thought. For over twenty minutes she brought old bedding out onto the hillside, then took it down to her mate's side. She pulled him a little further under the cover of the brambles, then covered him completely with the bedding, watched all the time by the other badgers, and us. Next she moved earth and stones from the hedgebank until there was nought to be seen but a burial mound, a barrow if you like.

She stood beside the grave for a while, head bowed. Then she turned and moved off into the darkness of the woods. Each of the watching badgers went to the graveside, then followed her into the woods.

It is impossible to write more about it. It was how it was. We could find no words then and went our way. A day or two later I put more stones and earth upon the little grave.

❄ ❄ ❄

Yellowhammers, the yellow buntings of open country, were feeding along the fields below the woods. Country ears interpret the bird's song as 'A little bit of bread and *no* cheese', and if one wants to hear it so, it is not too difficult. Yellowhammers are usually ground-feeding in flocks with other buntings and finches at this time of year.

We knew the yellowhammers as scribble larks when I was a lad, a name I eventually learned came from their pale eggs which have bold scribblings all over them. Occasionally, the eggs are clear, that is, unmarked. They are termed immaculate when like this. Many species which normally produce marked eggs will occasionally have clear clutches, or maybe one or two clear eggs in a clutch.

The bright yellow buntings, which are present all year round, are conspicuous among winter trees and as they move in flocks at this time of year they are even more easily observed than in summer. They are not as common as they were and I believe the numbers of most bird species are dropping. I am quite sure that the decline in barn owls, for example, is but a tiny part of the very real picture of falling populations of many British birds and animals.

A walk in the fresh air with a boisterous wind in open country makes for good bird-watching. Now that the cold winds are about again an extra layer or two of clothing does not go amiss. On a field trip recently I was surprised that some of our group were annoyed that we kept stopping to view the birds, finding it cold. But you can't watch wildlife when you're on the move.

Along the lane, which is mostly banked by steep hedgerows, there is just a yard or two of stone walling covered in spleenwort ferns and lichens. On the other side, tight in at the field edge, is an old slate-stone drinking trough of indeterminable age. Birds love it for it holds a few inches of rainwater and makes a fine birdbath, beautifully landscaped by Mother Nature with a green cascade of ferns on either side.

Wall pennywort loves to grow here, being a common plant in this part of Britain and quietly attractive with its circular leaves and summer spikes of greenish flowers. Lucky moon, corn leaves, penny caps, cups and saucers and cows are among the many country names. Corn leaves I know because it was a plant used against corns and warts but the origin of the Cornish name of cows is a mystery to me.

A huge sycamore grows in the bank here, along with oak, ash and Scots pine, an interesting mix of species much loved by the wildlife. Gaps in the hedge where dead elms fell are now refilling with beeches and oaks planted by the farmer.

Sycamore is capable of yielding sugar. Incisions used to be made in trees of forty to fifty years of age to let the colourless, transparent sap flow freely. The sap was evaporated by the heat of a fire, the residue being sweet, with a distinctive taste.

I recall this method of producing sugar being used by gypsies who had a small encampment in the parish of Fremington, in North Devon, during the war. Those were the days of rationing, but the gypsies lived well; they knew how to use the countryside in their way of life.

A covey of partridges, eight we counted, flew in from the higher ground above the valley in misty rain. We stepped back under cover to watch them land in the field but instead they dropped neatly onto the roof of a barn. There were shots in the distance and off the little birds flew again to curve in a wide arc and zoom into the cover of the hedge of Marsh field. On the run from the guns, probably, but here they were as safe as any wild creatures can be with a natural predator or two about as usual.

It is a surprise when birds seem to act out of habit. Partridges, as far as I know, rarely perch on landing, though I have seen them occasionally on stone walls. Birds that suddenly become aware they are a hunter's quarry do act out of the ordinary, I think, perhaps driven by some deeper instinct to go to any lengths to escape and survive. Would not we all change our normal routine if attacked and on the run?

Partridges are fine birds to watch, especially in summer in lazy, grassy fields, from a hedgebank with binoculars or telescope trained on a nest. It may be that one sees only head and neck for long periods, but one establishes a link of peaceful co-existence. Grasses and flowers waving in the breeze, butterflies moving by – such a rapport with nature sets a body wondering, realising these are special moments. They are enriching at the time and float back on the memory on a winter's night to be relived and cherished.

If I could have only one item for future use in the countryside it would be binoculars.

The magic world of the ditch never fails to turn up interesting, even amusing sightings. On a morning that seemed to be creeping hesitantly towards daylight Bracken was snuffling leaves and I saw a small dark shape break the line of dark green vegetation that marked the route of the ditch.

Puzzled for a moment at the jerky progress of the creature, I realised it was but the head of a moorhen. The bird was walking down in the ditch, which was shallow at this point, with its body and legs hidden from sight. Bracken suddenly saw it and stiffened, tail up, head on one side as the large-eyed head went on its jerky way along the field edge. Oh, for a video camera to record our sightings!

Moorhens are wonderful birds to study, for they take us into enchanting waterways. To see a moorhen perched on the lower branch of an alder tree overhanging the water is to want to wander quietly in these places and know more about them. From doing so we learn about dragonflies, damselflies, rushes, sedges and reeds, the flowers of wet places as well as other birds and mammals.

And just a mile away as the crow flies, on a faster-flowing waterway we heard a dipper singing as it perched on a midstream rock around midday. Its melody merged with the song of the stream, the two belonging together where winter sunlight gleamed deeply, burnishing the water and lighting the greenery beneath.

What need is there for more than this to gaze upon? No pathways laid with chippings or concrete pavements, please! Let the yielding of grass underfoot and mud on the shoes be part of the pleasure.

❄ ❄ ❄

The old lane is beautiful in its upkeptness, a place to revel in. Although man leaves this place alone, it is a manmade route: a lesson to us all. The spirits of farmers and of packhorse drovers are here, and maybe the faint echoes of children's laughter from the past, my own among them.

We stood by the stream at the lane end. 'Hark at the water, it is pleased to see us,' Endymion said. There was a definite welcome in the chattering like the bubbling laughter of Little People. John Clare was right:

The crows upon the swelling hills,
The cows upon the lea,
Sheep feeding by the pasture rills,
Are ever dear to me.

A buzzard was out over the slope below the woods, a descendant of those that were here when I was a lad, for they have been here for ever. The two crows which flew up from nowhere to harass it were performing a ritual followed for centuries by their ancestors. It is the thing to do if you are a crow: you chase buzzards.

A great arcing rainbow against grey clouds said rain was speeding in from the west though we were beneath blue sky. 'Wheeeoo!' The buzzard closed its wings, diving through the crows, for it had seen the coming rain and was off to shelter. It made sense. We were halfway up the lane when the rain hit, reminding us that leafless trees do not a shelter make. I could sense the many wild creatures grinning from their shelters as we hurried wet and muddy for home.

❄ ❄ ❄

Bill said he wanted to show me a beetle he had, indicating a rather large duffle bag. I asked him why the bag and not a matchbox and stepped back a pace. He told me the beetle was too big and just fitted the bag so I stepped back another pace, believing the real 'beast of Exmoor' was about to come to light.

But Bill took out a heavy wooden mallet of wondrous shape, fashioned directly from a knotted piece of timber.

'There now, that's beautiful, ennit?' he said, and it certainly was. All the natural strength of a complete piece of timber straight from the tree, no joins or joints but a solid piece.

Made from apple wood and bound with a steel band by the smithy once at Georgeham village long ago, the beetle was a treasure from days gone by, glowing with the vigour that well-used wooden objects often attain.

I discovered that the term 'beetle' comes from Beetley in Norfolk; the wood of which beetles or wooden mallets were often made came from crab-apple trees, which were common there.

It is said that the expression 'beetle-browed' comes from the habit of the tool to fray at the edges when in constant use and thus resemble fuzzy eyebrows. Wonderful stuff, this old country lore.

To handle the tool for five minutes or so was to handle a piece of country history. So many tools handmade by blacksmiths and other local craftsmen were purpose-made to fit a job and the user, from whatever was about; thus they had a character of their very own that even the best mass-produced items can never have, despite their modern strength and usefulness.

❄ ❄ ❄

Over the hard ground the hare was easy to see at first but as it came closer it seemed to vibrate, the whole of its outline becoming indistinct. Ghosting by foxes and hares is part of country lore. Here it was happening in front of our eyes. I could not fathom it out. Maybe it's that odd mix of colours that appear uniform until you obtain a clear view with binoculars, then you see every brown from sepia through to red and then some.

Into the bracken it went, a big hare, heavy in the coat, bigger than the faster hill hares but a beauty, sleek and dark about the back.

I could watch hares all day, save that they do not permit such close scrutiny for long. Hares by day, who knows what or who they may be in the light when the moon rises silver above the darkening woods.

Several wood pigeons came in fast across the field making for the woods, looking big in their low flight, the cold making them wilder as ever. Pigeons see exceptionally well and warn other creatures of your presence.

Wearing the right colours makes a huge difference when nature-watching. Army surplus stores are excellent places for country-coloured clothing. As it was, just the movement of binoculars being raised had the closest birds flying away to one side.

We did not see the hare again. Likely it was watching us. If a hare goes to hide it is rare to see it again, whereas a weasel, for example, will often come back to look and look again; quite curious little animals.

But the wind was biting. I thought of the lonely teapot we had left behind. It's happier pouring hot tea, so we took a vote and headed home.

❄ ❄ ❄

Lonely winds searched their way over the moorland, sighing among the bare boughs of winter trees where just a few hazels in a dip held catkins, swaying and golden. It was cold here on the high ground, and we hadn't seen a movement of wild creatures for half an hour. But there is a glow, an exhilaration, that comes from such a ramble and we knew there would be birds here and in the coombes when the weather warms.

Looking forward isn't 'wishing your life away', as some will have it. It's saying, 'We'll make the best of now and look for better.' That is spiritually a good thing.

A gust of wind moaned through the trees, but there were lambs on the farm at the end of the valley and the buzzard flying over knew its nest site for this year, I felt sure.

True, I wished the trees leafy again, but I'm sure the hawk did as well. There came a whirring sound of wings, at least so I thought, but a snowball plucked from snow and ice heaped against the hedgebank hit me amidships as I contemplated the leafiness to come. Laughter from behind the hedge. Two young people enjoying winter for what it is as more snowballs sailed too close for comfort.

You can combine winter reality with spring thoughts:

Old wishes, ghosts of broken plans,
A phantom hopes assemble,
And that child's heart within the man's,
Begins to move and tremble.

So I hoisted a snowball back, unerringly as it happened. Squeals came upon the cold air. Time to make a bolt for it.

I followed the buzzard along the moor track and beneath the beeches. Here were robins, blackbirds, more whizzing snowballs. ...

Winter is fine.

The old tree has been around for three or four centuries. Some dead branches are aerial logs really, supporting quite a different range of wildlife from old branches that have lain on the ground for a few years. Last summer there were bats about this tree, and many beetle burrows. Today a pair of great tits explore it. Already they are calling, the sound like the pumping up of a bicycle tyre.

In the dry ditch bridged by one of the fallen branches a bank vole clambered about the vegetation, its red fur helping us identify it. It took no notice of us – probably hadn't seen us – so we were able to watch it for a while as it hunted about, then stood and carefully groomed its coat.

Bank voles usually breed between April and October but the season may continue on in good weather with an abundance of seed food. They are often quite common in this area and I've found their skeletal remains in barn- and tawny-owl pellets many a time over the years. We have watched them on the top path in autumn and winter stripping the bark from elder trees to get at the cambium. Food is often stored at these times but on long summer days it's not unusual to observe bank voles about, and they are not difficult to watch closely.

As ever, the secret to such mammal-watching is to select a comfortable and secluded patch of wild habitat, sit very quietly and keep your eyes peeled. Let the creatures come to you. They will eventually, as long as you are not too noisy and don't wear very bright colours.

As the sun sank below the primitive landscape of Dartmoor where ancient man placed stones near the wonderful tors there came that awesome expectancy that has no obvious origins, just Mother Nature's signals to one's mind.

The deep pool here on the Dart begins as a rushing channel of white water over rocks, then somehow finds its peace beneath trees, stunted alders ready to leaf from already burgeoning buds. In a month it will be greener here, the oaks shading the tail of the pool, the favourite place for salmon peal when the daylight has gone and the sun gives way to the moon.

We were simply waiting for the moon, hadn't expected to see a largish bat appear as the only true earth satellite rose majestically from behind the wood. Silent in flight the bat flew rapidly about the pool's deep end, sometimes swooping in a glide, then flitting about in dancing circles as a bee might tell its comrades of rich pickings near by. Every fern and tree trunk, each stone in the landscape was either bathed in silver light or blackly silhouetted now.

Crashing, scratching and slithering sounds startled me. A black, writhing water creature my own body length appeared over the rocks and we relaxed again to watch the broken tree branch move gently on its way across the pool. Had we not seen the cause of the sounds, what pictures would the mind have conjured up as possible explanations? And a good thing too, for who knows what else it might have been in mankind's early days or nights (or even today).

A bat, a stick and moonlight. A couple of hours filled with beautiful memories. We are fortunate indeed to live in such a world, to live in the Westcountry, in fact.

Springtime

The rookery was busy in the late evening. Birds were back from their labours in the fields, happy to be in the ancestral homes built by their forefathers. No new nests here that I could see; the rooks, the DIY experts of the bird world, were keen to patch the old ones with fresh sticks.

'Quarr-quarr,' they called as we passed beneath the thirty or so nests. Away in the distance a song thrush called in the direction of Venus as we reached the tidal river.

It was a night of unusual colour and scenes, two men crossing the Taw at low tide, one pushing a bicycle. Sure of their passage, they waded to their knees from the area of fields at Pottington towards Fremington village, silver splashes and wide wakes where they walked, then over the twilit mudflats to leap onto saltings. A short cut indeed, the men primitive in their approach to the countryside as they passed cormorants drying their wings from fishing, black against yellow sky and mud the colour of otters.

Hooves pattering on grass: sheep running to watch Bracken trotting along the path above them. They followed him as far as the field would allow before it ended at wire fencing and they were forced to 'baa' after his white-tipped tail.

We counted more than fifty shelduck, these outnumbering the waders, for most have gone to breed. Two oystercatchers rolled and tumbled in the ebbing waters, enjoying a bath as a lone swan, as powerfully majestic as any eagle, honked its wings above us, low enough in the last light for us to see every detail. In a minute it would be passing our home, yet it would take us thirty more to get back there and put the kettle on.

* ❀ *

We were on a track that had barely changed since I was a boy. I used to come here in the dark of early mornings to pick mushrooms – such excitement for a lad! Even now, the birdsong and bees zooming along the hedgerows are exciting enough.

The track is the present leading to the future down in the valley, a timeless thing.

Timeless. And time doesn't matter here. We could put aside the hours and minutes, forget that man's time-linked life was once calculated by an archbishop to have begun at 9 am on 23 October 4004 BC. We could even forget our Mayan friends' belief that it will end on 22 December 2012 and just enjoy the holly blue butterflies hurtling headlong out of nowhere.

Such a richness of blue. Where were they going in such a hurry? Perhaps time has more meaning for them than we imagine. Just one perched on some holly long enough for us to see the small black spots on the pale blue undersides of its closed wings; then it was away again, chasing its friends.

The blues, hairstreaks and our one and only copper are all butterflies of the *Hycaenidae* family, swift flyers and some of our most beautiful insects.

Like so many of us in the Westcountry, I've grown up among butterfly-laden fields and hedgerows, the insects often abundant. But it was the green hairstreak that led me to study them more closely. I had not realised that my favourite colour existed on butterflies and will never forget really observing them on gorse for the first time.

The green hairstreak probably does well because its caterpillars have ten or more foodplants, which include gorse, broom and bramble: a handy factor in the battle for survival faced by all such creatures.

You don't see as many ring ouzels as you used to, so it was an absolute joy to find one in a coombe on my beloved Exmoor and later to see its mate join it from the streamside, where a miniature waterfall curtained their nest site. The male had been fairly obvious for a while but the female kept appearing and disappearing as if from nowhere; nowhere was a cranny hidden behind the water curtain of shining spray.

Ring ouzels – or mountain blackbirds as some call them – are interesting moorland birds, eating slugs, beetles and other insects as well as rowan berries when they are available. Once or twice when badger-watching I've heard them sing in the moonlight. Their song coupled with the hooting of owls is magic. Just once I caught sight of half a dozen, possibly a family, moving down off the moors on migration away to their wintering quarters, eating elderberries as they went. Juveniles at that stage look like heavily speckled young blackbirds.

Here in the Westcountry, Exmoor and Dartmoor are the last strongholds of the ring ouzel, but it is much more common in Wales and northwards throughout Scotland.

Here in the coombe a lone red admiral butterfly flew low along a sunlit slope, running the gauntlet of insect-eating birds but having no trouble as it fluttered inland helped by the breeze.

The leaves of bogbean showed in one wet area. Later the delicately pale flowers will light the marsh here. In Ireland the plant was used to purify the blood and the leaves to flavour beer, and as a general tonic. A very pretty flower and a useful one, growing at the bottom of a gorsy hillside where sheep and lambs ignored us as they lay enjoying the Exmoor sunshine.

For two weeks we'd been watching briefly at an old woodpecker's hole way up in a tree at the heart of a wood. A neighbour had seen 'a strange bird' coming out of the hole as she was passing by, so I'd said we would keep an eye open for it. Because the evening sunlight plays on the hole, it is well lit when we take Bracken for his last walk each day.

On 8 May, a very strange bird indeed flew from the hole at 8.30 pm, for the 'bird' was in fact a noctule bat. Off into the trees it flew on silent wings, followed by two more, all three flitting to catch insects in flight and, I feel sure, to hit the leaves with their wings to dislodge more.

Some time ago, I found a bat of this species on the ground where it had fallen during its first flight. Being born in a tree cavity does not allow for practice flights, so the first trial flight has to be successful, or the bat will likely die.

Now these three had gone into the trees of a private part of the woodland, undisturbed by people other than the owners.

On the path lay a bunch of limp bluebells. Someone had picked and then discarded them. A sad sight; far better to have left them where they were growing.

The celandines are still doing well, the late start bringing them brightly through May. They are having a glorious year, as are we for the seeing of them, along with the windflowers and the first of the wood sorrel.

Back home, the pipistrelle bats were out. Smaller than the noctules, these live in our roof space and are very welcome.

* ❀ *

Bill was in a chatty mood, telling of his early days working in the countryside. I learned that his father had been a hop-picker in Kent many years ago but had moved back to Devonshire after some ten years in the so-called 'Garden of England'.

Lots of dodges in those days, evidently. Hop-pickers would fill bushel measures quickly by not pushing them down hard and so bring in more bushels a day to the tally man. Picking wet hops in the early morning also meant filling bushels more quickly, apparently. Tough work, though, and often very cold.

It was the same with gamekeeping. Kill all the predators of game and do the job too well and you would soon be out of a job, so you left enough predators to hold your employment. It seems that the prey species and the gamekeepers looking after them were all dependent on the predators!

Bill spoke of the smaller but 'more interesting' villages of his youth. 'No need to ask what's wrong with the world,' he said. 'When the village was half the size, the church was always full. Today it's three times the size and the church is nearly empty.'

I didn't rack my brain over his mathematics, but knew what he said had truth in it. Change. An inevitability, but it is too fast these days, with little foresight applied. It has been the same with rapid urbanisation. Those who design and build the places wouldn't live anywhere near them. But there it is. People learn but they do little with their learning, sometimes, and nature pays the hard price all too often.

* ❀ *

I have found a length of stream where man has never trod, as they say. It runs under dense bushes and trees with just one area open to the sunlight. It's a lovely spot away from the madding crowd. A moorhen's nest with five eggs tells of the seclusion and, sitting very quietly, I soon pick up on five different bird species feeding young or with nests in a matter of fifty metres.

Lovely, these green secluded places with chattering water and not a bit of litter in sight. It's like going back in time, for I can see to the bottom of the pool and watch minnows. Paradise! Ramsons, the lovely wild garlic, grow all along one bank. At night they will light the place. Jack-by-the-hedge and yellow archangel grow where woodrush has not established itself as firmly as in most places.

Honeysuckle twines among the saplings across the stream, the leaves having been showing since January. It has to be one of the loveliest of plants. It flowers in June and on through the summer, unbelievably lovely and sweet-scented. Used medicinally against asthma, lung problems and headaches, the woodbine has been much loved by countryfolk for centuries. They say its flowers placed in a girl's bedroom will bring her dreams of love. I wonder what boys used?

And groundsel. Where do you not find it? The plant I saw was probably wood groundsel for it was bushier altogether with deeply toothed leaves. Gardeners may not like it but it's a pretty plant and was a well-known poulticing herb in its day. Also used as a cure for the staggers disease in horses. Nowadays groundsel makes a useful feed for rabbits and canaries and is well liked by both.

* ❀ *

Sunshine after rain: is there a better time to be out in the country? Fresh smells and summer sounds and here, looking down over the wooded valley of Horner, not far from Stoke Pero, it was Paradise Found.

We had rounded a bend to the left of the ridge over the river to be confronted with a moving tapestry of gentle colours on a green background. Lush ferns everywhere, mossy trees, black-and-white movement of two pied flycatchers and, walking slowly away, five red deer hinds in no hurry at all. Grey wagtails chased insects from bank to bank of the sparkling waters under the trees, a sight of sheer beauty in the dappled sunlight. Enchanted was the only word for it.

I could not spoil it by raising my binoculars to observe more closely. Anything the slightest bit 'technical' would have marred this picture of Mother Nature's design. A lovely world.

From here to Cloutsham along the Horner Water is a lovely walk on a day like this, the stream rushing down the coombe to Bossington, filled with rain off the higher moors; not a force to be played with. Only a mile or so away is Luccombe, 'the valley shut in by hills', and a pretty village with an interesting church.

Wonderful walking country this, rich in wildlife. It's well worth getting on those walking shoes and exploring, for this is fine country for seeing deer and dippers, the two favourite d's of Exmoor.

It was not hard to imagine that wolves once roamed here, no real threat to man but destroyed nevertheless, perhaps because man wanted the deer for pleasure and meat but did not want the competition.

Then a cuckoo called from Stoke Ridge way and continued calling. Magic. Like the sound of the greenshank's call, or the curlew's, there is a wild freedom in its calling.

Second Summer

A summer morning watching the sun come up. It was a gentle dawn with birdsong rather muted, perhaps by the mist wandering aimlessly along the valley floor, sending out wraiths like messengers winding around the trees to tell them it was daytime.

I believe there are people who have never seen a sunrise. It seems a pity, for it is a moving spectacle, whether seen over hills and moors, above rooftops or in a garden. A tonic to begin the day with.

Bracken went out onto the saltings to hide in the grass, black butterfly ears listening all I could see of him; this is one of his games. I poked around at a creek edge then under a tide tunnel and along the inland creek, scattering a dozen rabbits that had come out with the dawn light. The hawthorns by the water are lovely now in blossom; May in June, fine trees.

A kestrel flew from one of these. Had it stayed still I wouldn't have seen it within the canopy of dense foliage. On flickering wings it flew into the woods on the steep hillside, such a narrow strip of trees but all important as wildlife habitat. These are mostly slow-growing oaks with a mix of ash and other trees, great for wildlife, both residents and migrants.

The fields and woods are full of summer now, late bluebells vying with early yellow flag to be noticed and there in the mud the prints of badger and moorhen clearly recognisable, telling a story of creatures hid somewhere close by. Indeed, suddenly hearing both moorhen and pheasant calls, I looked up to see Bracken grinning from the top path. The hiding and watching game had turned to tag, played with anything that moved.

A male stickleback was performing the zigzag dance, to and fro in front of the female, waiting for her signal to move in and enjoy their mutual moments of egg releasing and fertilisation.

The stream pool under the alders here is a green magical place at this time with swathes of meadowsweet leaves telling of the creamy whiteness to come, and of the perfume mingling with the hawthorn's last blossom around midsummer.

The male stickleback looked rather splendid, the clear water allowing glimpses of blue eyes and red belly. These were three-spined sticklebacks, their spawning taking place in their little nest of weed and algae, cemented with a sticky kidney secretion. He would chase off all intruders while keeping busy fanning a water current down to the nest to ventilate the eggs. A tough little life, but with a bit of luck and clean water, the young will survive.

Fascinating stuff, the life of fishes. Their ways vary so much between species, you will soon realise that nothing about nature is boring. If you think soaps on the TV are the slightest bit interesting, get to grips with Mother Nature instead and really live.

About a hundred yards along the bank, a grey heron was fishing. The large bird stood on a shingle area, only its feet covered by water. But as it's a sharp bend, there is a deepish pool where fish are often to be found. We watched it make a few tentative jabs but, if anything, it was getting a drink rather than having success fishing. Another five minutes and it gave up, great wings flapping to lift it up and away to fly downstream either to a more amenable pool or the estuary.

The male chaffinch was noisy with his calling, proclaiming that he and his mate had a nest near by. It took a while to locate for it was built neatly into a tree fork, colours matching to perfection.

Chaffinches nested in this tree when I was a boy. The tree's girth, like my own, is larger now than then. I had a silly mind picture of a magician sawing me in half to count the growth rings as one does with trees. It must have been the fruit pastille I'd just had to quell my thirst; powerful stuff, the green ones!

Endymion and Robin decided it was a good place to eat our sandwiches. Mind you, the idea had crossed their minds a few times within half an hour of leaving home. Our scattered crumbs enticed the chaffinch down. He was splendid in breeding colours. The female followed, better matching her surroundings; a handsome pair. We could sit back, relax and watch these lovely birds from close to.

It was hereabouts I'd first learned to love wildlife, the old tree part of those years. Now another generation was enjoying both tree and chaffinches. I was bridging the gulf of years via the simplest of pleasures, those of Mother Nature giving freely.

Still common, the chaffinch loves to be among trees, living mainly on plant seeds and insects. If you listen carefully to the song you may notice marked differences from bird to bird even though the pattern of sound is recognisable. Just as with ourselves across the country, regional dialects have been noted.

I distinctly heard our two chatting: 'Well, that's all the food us'll get out of these people, me 'andsome.'

'Yes, I'll get back on the eggs and you carry on singing then, me dearie. Us'll 'ev five mouths to feed come Tuesday.'

There, in the dry grassland dell sheltered on three sides by rocks, grew kidney vetch, doing its best to stand upright on spindly stems that would have been glad of a drop of rain. Though its English name suggests it could cure kidney disease, the vetch was truly famed as a herb to heal wounds, along with yarrow and one or two others. Here its golden colour rivalled even the gorse growing just above it, though it may be found with orange or even purple tinges and I've seen it a creamy white occasionally. Local names include fingers and thumbs, lamb's foot and butterfingers. You may well see bumble-bees forcing open the long petals to reach the rich source of nectar within the flower. If you do, stop and watch one of these friendly old characters of flowery, grassy places, for they endear themselves to the caring observer.

Cow parsley, or Queen Anne's lace, is almost over now, for it gets out and about early in April and usually sees in Midsummer along with the fairies. Quite harmless to mankind, it is sometimes fed as greens to rabbits and is the true pea-shooter plant of country youngsters. Catch someone on the back of the ear with haw from a cow parsley pea-shooter and you've a friend for life.

Alexanders is still about, too, showing quite yellow and very common in parts of the Westcountry, where it loves seaside areas. A good herb with all parts edible, it has been used against flatulence, snake bites and stomach chills and is good as a parsnip substitute as well as in salads. So if you get the wind up from being bitten by a snake, Alexanders is the answer for you. A herb of Macedonia in Alexander the Great's country.

Most visitors to Dartmoor miss its true beauty by driving around in the hours twixt 10 am and 6 pm. A Dartmoor evening when the coombes are in purple shadow and the setting of the sun spreads its golden light to turn the Dart and Taw or Walkham rivers into molten gold is when to be there, for then time is meaningless and the spirit is all.

A trout splashing in the Walkham becomes an alchemist as it turns the water drops to liquid gold. Add that to any birdsong and you have the magic of the moors. Or on a moonlit night let Merrivale enchant you with its rugged grandeur and wonderful standing stones of ancient healers; or on a day of gentle mists when the muted song of a robin lifts the heart, be there.

The moorland plants, their shape and size dictated by the wild conditions, are no less beautiful for being small and, after all, the closer you have to look the closer to nature you will be.

Even the sphagnum has so many colours, while cinquefoil and lousewort hug the ground knowing it is their home, just as the ponies know, and the sheep who face up to us and stamp their feet, laying claim to the land.

Follow a tumbling stream into a summer-filled gorge to sit where ancient peoples sat, watching the same dragonfly species as we do today. Timeless, yes, and nameless, for if you lose yourself to the feel of the place you might be on Exmoor, Bodmin, or in the Scottish Highlands, time and place being merely the now and the where you stretch happily weary legs. Irresistible places. If you cannot visit them, read, for there is a timelessness within a book, equally beautiful.

Along the ancient country lane in a green shade grows hogweed; tall and robust, lovely to see, it gets its name from the fact that it was once gathered as pig food. Once believed to have medicinal value, the young leaves were a popular delicacy, tasting not unlike asparagus when boiled. From now to late summer you may see the bright orange soldier beetles on the white umbels of its flowers. I would suggest you treat the plant with some caution, especially in hot weather, as it contains a volatile substance which may irritate sensitive skin. This is true of both the common and the giant hogweed.

We found a robin's nest near by with five young in it, an adult busily collecting food for her babes.

Yellow pimpernel grew in the gateway under the trees at the wood edge. It is the first I've seen in flower this year. Often it blooms in May. The late spring probably held up quite a few flowers but they come through eventually to give us joy and maybe to provide their healing powers. Yellow pimpernel was used as a painkiller though its relative, creeping jenny, was the more used healing herb and popular as a garden plant.

Lovely to see rosebay willowherb in flower again too – such colour! – along with foxgloves. One is filled with emotion and good feelings at such glorious sights; how lucky we are.

We have a great deal to look after and hang on to; we must try, for the sake of each and every species. The latest news on global warming is alarming, but it was known about for a long time. As I've said umpteen times, if we mess about with Mother Nature she'll teach us a very hard lesson.

Convinced it is summer, we clambered up a very steep hillside to the top of a hanging oak wood when, like a light going out, the sunlight disappeared, it became quite dark and the heavens opened. Fortunately the dense canopy did its umbrella job very well for the time it took to find an overhang formed by some minor landslip erosion. There was ample room and even a large log to sit on.

Then it dawned on me: the log had been placed as a seat. It had not fallen here naturally. This was some youngster's den, or had been, with ivy at one side forming a useful curtain-cum-hide.

Beyond the curtain of ivy the rain now formed its own curtain of water in front of us. It was like being behind a waterfall. I could not believe our luck to have found this shelter, just to sit in dry clothing inches from the downpour.

'Time to search about,' said Endymion, who looks for every movement or opportunity to see yet another wild creature or plant. I must admit to being enchanted by the storm and its power, watching soil and leaf debris, even sizeable sticks shooting beneath bushes as tiny rivers formed.

'Look, a moth here. There are always lovely moths to find.'

On the tree trunk forming one side of the cave was a brown moth, delicately marked and well camouflaged: a lobster moth, a pale form, for there are dark forms of the species. It is the caterpillar which gives the insect its name; when disturbed it takes on the appearance of a lobster, even rearing its head and tail up over its body. A good find on a wet summer's day.

Gosh! August the first: what happened to July? Brooklime showed blue near the water, the glossy green leaves growing in pairs, the flowers from two short stalks coming from the stem opposite each other. A quick search around revealed lesser spearwort, a member of the buttercup family, and watercress, which likes it here where the water is just about on the move.

There were a few common sympetrum dragonflies about, two of the males having very bright scarlet bodies. Watching these, my attention was caught by movement underwater where a collection of small pond snails seemed to be pushing along. Crouching to watch these minute shells, all gathered in one spot, I realised I was looking at a caddis case, the protective silky tube of the larvae armoured by the shells attached to it.

Sometimes caddis larvae use bits of stick or broken plant stems, even sand grains, thus building their homes of different debris, their choice often depending on the species of caddis fly. At first sight, adult caddis flies look like moths, but on examination you will find hairs, not scales, on the wings.

A nudge from Bracken and I dipped my binoculars in the pool trying to regain my balance. Redfield binoculars are very well waterproofed, by the way. If you're going pond-dipping they are the ones to use.

Water mint was in flower. It should be around now until October Good against earache, it was also used as smelling salts and, strewn about floors, as a beautifully perfumed air-freshener several centuries ago. Nature provides, man copies. In wet places, water mint is quite common. It was thought to have been cultivated by the Romans to be used in cooking, but it's said the practice goes back to the Stone Age.

I mentioned watercress yesterday, but only rather fleetingly. Almost a disservice, for it is a superb healing plant, one of nature's many wonders. It is high in vitamins and minerals, a nourishing tonic for those in stress and increases vitality. I'd better get some.

It is said the Egyptian kings gave their slaves watercress to increase their productivity. Now you know how the pyramids were really built. Watercress also dissolves stones and gravel. (Obviously the Egyptians did not rub the pyramids with it when built.) As an antiseptic it can be used as a poultice for wounds, ulcers, boils and other skin infections, including cold sores. The juice mixed with vinegar is said to relieve lethargy.

Watercress in your salad sandwiches, then; it draws the vital health elements from the earth, a great tonic. But, just as a precaution, it is wise not to eat watercress growing in areas close to sheep. It is believed that some problems, like liver fluke, can pass into humans via the droppings.

Always better to be safe rather than sorry; the sensible way forward.

It is coming up to that time of the year for wasp stings. Dab on a raw cut onion and put a slice on the sting. Excellent. Headaches come at any time. Again, you can use an onion, inhaling or applying it direct (grated in a poultice or halved and held to the head). Raw or cooked onions reduce blood pressure. And you thought it was an apple a day that kept the doctor at bay.

There you go – watercress, onions and a bit of parsley to chew and you'll be as perky as they make 'em. Mind you, a wasp sting in the right place can get rid of lethargy too.

Mother Nature has done a good job with the woodland. Old trees have fallen to lie in state while others lean against some that are young and strong. Regeneration can be seen here and there is the promise of trees to come, while bramble and bracken grow on the slopes along with dog roses.

It was here we found a prize indeed. High brown fritillaries, quite uncommon and an unexpected bonus. To see the females laying eggs on dog violet leaves bodes well for next summer. This fritillary species can be identified by silver spots inside the red markings on the underside of the hind wings, quite different from the common dark green fritillary.

Late July into August was becoming an exciting time, the finding of an uncommon species the reward of those who are able to spend time in the field. The bramble, thistles and bracken here were keys to the species' success and survival, as are the violets as food plants for the caterpillars.

At different places along the wood edge bramble flowers vary considerably in colour, from almost white to a very strong pink. Come blackberry time the fruits will be quite different on some of these bushes, there being numerous blackberry types; they say four hundred or more in Britain alone.

Warm sunshine, rare breeding butterflies, the promise of blackberries to come, enough to fill any country-lover's day. And then we found several green lacewings in the dog rose patch. This summer's generation was taking nectar and eating tiny insect prey, enjoying supper then washing it down with the nectar, just as we might. Their translucent wings are beautiful, but look closer to see the large glowing eyes of this lovely insect as the yellow evening sunlight glints on them.

If you have visited Fingle Gorge near Moretonhampstead recently you may have seen a family of kestrels there, five hovering together, a splendid sight even for those of us who live in the Westcountry and are used to seeing kestrels, buzzards and the like.

Moreton, originally called Moor-town, was once famous for its Dancing Tree or Cross Tree, a pollarded elm of some note, now long gone. Evidently boards were placed in the branches and people actually danced and played music in the tree.

Some four years ago, otters were playing below Dunsford bridge here on the Teign river and no doubt this lovely river is rich in wildlife of all kinds. Chudleigh Glen, which runs into the Teign, is a pixie haunt with an area well known as Pixie Parlour, and there is lovely bird-watching hereabouts. At Teignmouth 'tis said that dwarf elder (found about the cliffs of the area) grows only where the battles of Saxons and Danes took place; hence an old name for this plant: Dane's elder.

We found hemlock growing here, too. Hare's parsley, gypsy curtains and Devil's blossom are but three of the names given to this beautiful but dangerous plant. When goats and donkeys eat it they fall into a strange, death-like sleep from which they eventually awaken. It was certainly curtains for Socrates, who is said to have taken a fatal potion of hemlock. So if you see it about, avoid it other than to admire its beauty. A pretty plant, hemlock is also known as lady's lace and lady's needlework.

Lovely to see hemp agrimony in flower now, pink and fluffy, and also the golden agrimony or Aaron's rod, which makes good wine and a tea against evils and poisons. I wonder if that's why it's growing here, next to hemlock.

Quiet moorland, a hint of give in the ground telling of a high water table; a boot-sucking place in winter, but more friendly today. Glints of bluetails and scarlet damselflies by a dark-water pool. They've been here for unimaginable years, no doubt part of the moorland history, part of the very nature of this place.

A dead crow close to a stone wall – death as much a part of nature as life – already helping life as two black and orange burying beetles conduct their own funeral service for the bird.

Wheatears, whinchats and redstarts were in the coombe; family parties, some of the birds merely weeks old but already building up strength and energy for journeys of thousands of miles over vast oceans and land masses.

Some years ago I found wheatears nesting in a tin wedged in a wall. Odd nest sites this year include that of spotted flycatchers who had nested in an old blackbird's next, using the old nest as a platform for their own smaller one. Perhaps the oddest was that of the bluetits who built in an upside-down plant pot, a foot-high one of clay, the birds going in and out through the drainage hole.

Then Bracken's ever-questioning nose disturbed a shrew from its hiding place at the foot of a gatepost where moorland touches farmland. The shrew zigzagged away; a fine little creature, yet old superstitions credit shrews with evil influences on man and beast. In fact, people were so barmy about this that they would bore a hole in an ash tree, thrust in a live shrew and plug it up. A twig from this 'shrew ash' was said to cure people or animals who were shrew-stricken. Pity the poor shrew, I say.

Six am. The rising sun sends golden light along the hill fields on the other side of the river, the dips casting their own shadows of blue-green. A collared dove, my early morning call, is persistent in its praise of the day.

Along the top path leaves are more colourful than the lovely pink flowers, rich autumn colours too early for that season. Above me in the oaks a squirrel rubs its eyes, scratches its tummy and yawns. It is that 'Disney' time of day, straight out of *Bambi*, when you can actually watch the awakening of day creatures. I check the hollow tree as I pass quietly beneath and sure enough a tawny owl perches, dozing after its night out.

In the wood, cow-wheat shows its lovely yellow flowers. It arrives late in bloom here on the north-facing slopes yet I know places where it blooms in May. They say that pregnant women who eat flour from its seeds will bear male children. 'Cow'-wheat because cattle like it and are said to give only the finest milk and butter when they eat it. The plant has dark wheat-like seeds.

However, this is very much a woodland plant and not common, its presence here telling of old woods of great wildlife interest. Its scientific name, *Melampyrum pratense*, suggests a plant of the fields, *pratense* meaning 'growing in meadows', so maybe it was more widespread years ago.

Bracken drinks from the healing waters of the old dripping well, triggering thoughts that a mug of tea would go down well now. We wander up the hill path together under the trees in perfect space, not a soul about. The early riser gets the best of the day.

✳ ✪ ✳

August rain brings honey and wine, they say. Could be right; rain swelling the fruits to be ripened by the sun though, no doubt, the wine referred to is from grapes rather than blackberries or elder. The dew has been heavy at times. Nice to see the jewel-like glints on early morning grass with blackbirds shuffling in it for a bath.

In a little café in town the aroma of coffee was enticing and on a Friday market day, with the streets packed and bustling, to wander in was instinctive. The coffee wasn't too bad, either. Now here's some weather lore to have you watching every cup of coffee you drink: bubbles collecting in the centre of the cup are a sign of fair weather, but when they form around the sides as a ring, expect rain. So there you go. All those satellites and weather forecasters, and all you need do is make a cup of coffee and stare at it.

The bubbles in my cup were all over the place. Changeable weather. It was raining outside but a watery sun shone through the grey. A daddy-long-legs tapped at the window. I showed it my cup and it flew on, happy that the rain would soon cease. It did, so we went home along the riverbank.

The brilliance of the year is fading already. There is a more subdued, mature feel about the year; quieter without the birdsong, less exuberant, but remaining summerish. The woods are still but the birds are nurturing their young; feeding family parties flitting through the trees, silent, busy. Food has to be found. No cash sales here to make life easy – seek and find or perish. Tough world.

✳ ✪ ✳

As late summer merges into autumn the mewing cries of a young buzzard perched in the oaks tell of a bird not yet independent enough to hunt for itself. At least that's what it's telling its parents. It has been a good vole and mouse year and there are rabbits aplenty, but the hawk will have to learn that the latter are about mainly at dawn and dusk and not at midday.

It's breakfast or supper, or a bit of scavenging if it wants midday lunch.

We sat on cushions of woodrush, which grows well here under the oaks. Looking out across the sheep-grazed open field we could see hawkweed growing tall and yellow along the field edge, an interesting plant which may baffle beginners in botany for the pictures of it in books often differ slightly from the actual plant.

Thanks to a process called apomixis most of the seed is produced without fertilisation, each plant giving rise to a line of true-breeding descendants. Thus all hawkweed plants in one locality will look the same, yet differ from those in another locality. About three hundred hawkweed species are recognised by botanists in Britain alone. But don't worry about it; even the experts have problems telling them apart. Be happy knowing it is hawkweed.

Why hawkweed? Long ago it was thought that hawks ate the plants to obtain the milk-like juice and that this gave the birds their sharp eyesight. Maybe they do. Lovely country lore.

A shadow glided along the floor of the wood. Above us an adult buzzard screamed, the young hawk in the trees answering, shifting from one foot to the other. In the talons of the great brown bird hung a dead rat, clearly visible, so the youngster's cries had not been in vain.

The stream is busy here, springing out of the rich green gloom of the hazel spinney over green-mossed stones, filling the quiet dark pools with its twirling, bubbling currents. Then on it leaps into the sunlit meadow, swirling beneath the fruit laden branches of elder swaying in the breeze. From here it becomes a ribbon of silver light where the bank is always golden with flowers: early in the year comes coltsfoot, then marsh marigolds and buttercups, now ragwort. Always golden, even in winter with the gorse; summery all the year round.

A stick spins in the current, sweeping into the sepia water under the bridge arch, the stream whispering in the secret lair beneath the curving stones brought from some nearby quarry, then bursting into song and sunlight flows over flat stones, the places of stone loach or gudgeon.

Rusty iron of old sluice machinery hidden in the grass where two ancient Bramley apple trees tell of an orchard long gone, and the tottering stone wall and a hunk of timber of an old mill. No more the creaking sounds of waterwheel, just the creaking of my back as I clamber over and into a lane which once held the footprints of packhorses.

Then the ferny banks: buckler, hart's tongue, hard fern and polypody. All is green save for the breast colour of a robin on the stile top and sunlight on a tree. Its solitary song seems to make the silence more profound.

Autumn and Winter

Mother Nature is at her best here, where no one abuses the magic she works. Leaving such a place alone is not neglect; it is respect for her.

Sea trout surging upriver and snipe coming in to a little marsh. I love the few little snipe bogs that remain in the area despite so much land drainage. Just three snipe dropping into rushy cover as I negotiate the tussocky clumps to avoid sinking. Gosh, it's good to feel give in the ground in a dryish summer; green here, though the hills around are brown-looking.

You used to see snipe rising like leaves scattered by autumn winds once upon a time, lifting up from underfoot, a quick 'skaark' and down they'd dip or zigzag high upon the breeze and higher till they reached the trees. Snipe are pretty birds. There's no better word to describe them, with their attractive plumage and gentle faces. Seen through binoculars they are pretty, and I for one love to watch them.

This must be fairy ground. It is just right. Hawthorn and elder, masses of ferns, springs of fresh water and moss cushions. There is a row of quartz stones, pinkish and glimmering with shiny bits, all across the field by the hedge. If you search there are more hidden by grasses.

On to the next field, where one of the best-looking, ricketiest gates I've ever seen just asks to be painted and sketched. Man makes a gate, smart and new; nature and use fashion it into this beautiful green, grey and brown mossy wooden creature who grunts and groans in rough weather or leans against its posts, to be leaned on and trusted. Still it does its job of holding back stock or letting them through as bidden, held by a rusty catch. I stroke the top bar. The gate moves, leaning against me, glad of company, a good friend.

Cock-brumble, Lady Garten berries and brummelty kites: all colourful country names for the bramble, showing the affinity with the plant that country folk have always had.

The value of bramble as a medicinal herb, a source of fruit and refreshing tea, dates back to early man, for blackberry seeds were found in the stomach of Neolithic people found in Essex claypits.

Today brambles are often destroyed in woodlands, yet they are an important source of food and shelter for wildlife, a point that should be remembered from the point of view of nature conservation. This lovely member of the rose family should be revered for its beauty and usefulness, never looked upon as a nuisance value shrub as it so often is. One of these days, we may well be more glad of it than we now appreciate.

It is lovely to see hedge-nuts again on the hazel, and what better-tasting apple is there than one straight off the tree in September? From the tenth of this month to 19 November is autumn, by the way.

But listen now for what is called the 'second spring', that lovely time when song thrushes sing along with chiffchaffs, the latter soon to migrate for their winter holidays. Do try to catch this moment of the year and look for brimstone butterflies and dog violets, even as autumn begins to tinge the trees.

Check your calendar for the harvest moon. The moon will last a few days. If there are fine nights at this time, go out and watch for the flights of migrating flocks of songbirds across the moon. Sometimes you can even hear them calling. Now that is country magic. A September night out of doors takes some beating.

All the way along the water we could see brown trout moving as swift shadows in the depths. A 'water' in this area is somewhere between a stream and a river, and many are named such. Years ago when I asked a farmer how a water is named, he told me that you can leap across a stream, you would not even contemplate leaping a river, but a water is one of those you might try leaping if you were desperate to get over – not otherwise. Technical stuff.

I love watching trout. They can vary in colour according to their environment, and even the flesh can vary from white to pink depending whether you find them in lakes or some mountain tarn. Tiny fish in a good trout water may be under threat as trout are carnivores whose diet may change seasonally depending on food availability.

A trout swims by, moving its tail from side to side. If chasing prey or being pursued by predators, trout can reach speeds of up to ten metres a second. That's fast.

Trout hatcheries where fertilised eggs and young are reared in large numbers are not a new idea. The practice is referred to as long ago as the 1700s.

Other fish species are not the main part of the trout's diet, for they take aquatic insects and their larvae, molluscs and crustaceans in large numbers. The brown trout is one of the two forms of the species *Salmo trutta*. The other form is the seat trout, which migrates from the fresh water where it hatches to the sea, and returns to fresh water to breed.

Sit by a Westcountry waterway and you'll see a wealth of wildlife, especially if you're close to woodland. Then you'll be enjoying one of the richest habitats of all. Happy nature-watching.

Had we not seen a cat in the field staring up at us through the trees, we wouldn't have stopped. Something odd about its mouth, I thought, and training binoculars on it saw that it held at fat mouse by the head, the creature's body and tail dangling below the predator's chin. Then, leaning on the fence overlooking the field, I spied the round, ball-like shape of a dormouse nest in a shrub directly beside us. The nest was neatly made of grass, honeysuckle bark and leaves, the summer nest of this animal. No doubt it was inside, fast asleep until nightfall.

Dormice make their winter nest down a hole in a bank, or under a tree stump or tree-root system, where they hibernate. October will be the beginning of their hibernation until the spring. Good to find them here. Years ago, a dormouse rolled out of its hiding place, a crevice I happened to use as a steadying point on a cliff path where a few of us were walking. I caught it as it fell, had a quick look and put it back in its 'snug', still in the deep torpor of hibernation sleep.

Quite a few grasshoppers about in a few places, so they seem to have had a good year generally. We have some in the garden, which is an unusual pleasure, one which I hope will continue.

I heard the chirping of males and then a brown-coloured one flew on to the windowsill in full view, a common grasshopper. This species' female will lay long narrow eggs in holes in the ground, the holes having been made by the strong ovipositor at the tip of her body. Lovely insects.

If there is a bird more a part of the white waterways which splash their way to the sea than the dipper, then I do not know of it. Watching dippers, you can imagine that these crystal-clear streams first spawned them, that the very first Adam and Eve of dippers came from primeval waters and have never left them. Certainly, to walk a typical dipper stream here in the Westcountry and not find any brings on a sense of foreboding. There are meant to be dippers in such places.

Dripping, lichened rocks could not be greener than here beneath the trees, wonderful splashy places with friendly shadows and liquid diamonds falling from smooth rocks and narrow ledge. If I could choose, this would be the scene from my study window: light and shade, green of moving ferns and mosses cushioning tree roots thrusting from rich soil.

Then a dipper flew by upstream, not stopping – but a dipper all the same – and all was well with the day.

Standing by a pebbly beach with its shallows and deeps, I watched the shining wet leaves of hart's tongue bobbing as a spring watered it from above, bobbing as do dippers and wagtails, part of the water motion. A smaller fern clasping the rocky walls at head height was wall rue, an evergreen once known as white maidenhair and taintwort, the latter name from its use as a remedy for rickets or the taint, as it was called.

Dippers, ferns and rushing water in a secret dell, what more can one ask? Maybe a cheese sandwich and a drink but, all in all, the gods had given us a lot to be thankful for. It was a place where I could be content for the rest of my days, as mankind once was, in rapport with nature.

The warm old wall of the farmhouse had attracted a mass of cluster flies (*Pollenia rudis*), who would soon be ready to crawl into crevices to hibernate.

It is the time of year when the hedgehogs are having a last fling, too: they seem to show themselves more now than at any time. The farmer says three were in the yard last night, perhaps a late family party to lay up fat for the long winter sleep. Mark you, a warm sunny day may wake up a hedgehog. They'll emerge to change nests sometimes if this happens, hibernation being deeper the colder it is.

The signal to hibernate will likely be the first frosts, the very frosts that kill off the worker wasps, which at the moment have a craving for sugar and may be found busy at windfall apples or damaged fruit in the trees.

Quite a few flowers about. I found wild angelica in bloom in damp places close to the ditch line. Probably the last of the cow parsley family to be about, it is a froth of white tinged with pink and very lovely. In one area a purple colour dominates, the divided leaves swollen where they join the stem.

Lovers of cake will know the variety that is crystallised and used as a cake decoration, yet the true wild plant was widely eaten itself as a candy, as well as being an angelic plant and healer for many ailments: a universal remedy in fact.

The plant spreads or migrates by its wind-dispersed seeds, the flattened, oval fruits having thin wings that take them about the countryside seeking damp places. Look for it in such habitats or on cliff tops and wet woods, where it is often common and always beautiful.

There was lemon peel at the bottom of the lane, neatly peeled from the fruit and just lying there, fairly fresh. I couldn't see anyone about and Bracken was busy working out what scents were whose, so the citrus-lover must have been way up ahead of us. I could have understood orange peel, as oranges are popular enough fruit, but either the person in front had far less sensitive taste-buds than mine or they were wandering about with screwed-up eyes.

Mind you, lemons are good news as a tonic, an antiseptic and a diuretic. (I had a vision of a vigorous person with hygienically clean insides rushing for the nearest bushes, his or her eyes screwed tight shut!) Seriously, though, add lemon juice to three cloves and some honey in hot water and you have as good a treatment as any for coughs, colds, even flu.

Russian country folklore recommends that after the age of forty we take the juice of one lemon and one orange in hot water every morning as a way of preventing arteriosclerosis. The Romans used lemons as an antidote to all poisons.

Almost as yellow and white as the lemon peel, two grey wagtails who live here the year round chased autumn insects at the edge of the stream formed by surface water run-off and a few springs. It is a pretty place, made prettier by autumn's warm colourings, a nip in the air reminding us of the time of year.

The wagtails' roost is in a sort of cave formed by the stonework of a bridge and the adjoining gatepost, sheltered by dense vegetation. We have observed them going in of a late evening just before sunset; a good spot.

The walk between Woody Bay and Hunters Inn on an autumn evening can be blissful. I was dropped off at the car park and soon heading westwards with Bracken happily up ahead, under trees for a while, passing a fox earth then out on to the open path. Gorse, ling, bell heather and cross-leaved heath glowed purple and gold to our left, and the sea and the Welsh coastline were to our right, lights coming on in Wales as the first stars and Venus shone in the dimming sky.

Under trees goldenrod was still in flower, along with the deep yellow cow-wheat, a much deeper yellow form here than in the woods behind our home, where it is quite pale. Goldenrod (*Solidago virgaurea*) flowers quite late hereabouts; the books usually say July to August. A wound-healing plant for both internal and external use, it is said to have cost half a crown an ounce in Elizabethan times, so highly regarded was it.

Three buzzards soared overhead, the rather rapid cries of one telling it was a youngster remaining for a while with its parents.

No visitors about now, only two people passing by as we headed down the curving path that cuts away from the sea to drop steeply towards the inn hidden beneath dense woodland. Here a tawny owl hooted and many bats flew in the darkening sky, the most I've seen for some time.

Gulls were flying to roosts in the cliffs from inland. Earlier in the year they had nested on the ledges, laying eggs in precarious-looking places. Herring gulls, who may live for twenty to thirty years, usually lay three eggs. Not a bad life in an area as lovely as the Westcountry.

Rooks are calling in the trees just over the hilltop. Occasionally one will fly up into view and drop back again out of sight. If I didn't know better I'd say they had a trampoline and were playing in the tree-tops. Another comes up, flicks its black wings and drops back, to a chorus of raucous cheers. They do have a trampoline. Content with this decision I walk on downhill the other way so as not to spoil the illusion.

Pigeons are flocking, clattering away in an arc as is the way of pigeons. The dark soil shows up their droppings here, telling of the roost along with a few feathers scattered about. Then a tighter circle of feathers, these plucked by a sparrowhawk having lunch.

A light rain hit my neck. Hunching my collar up and pushing my binoculars beneath my old Barbour to keep them dry, I watched plough furrows take on the shine of wetness, turning the colour of the reflected sky, from brown to blue-grey, the field like some chameleon in its changing.

Then a hare rose before me as he caught sight of Bracken, looking him in the eye instead of running. 'Daft thing,' Bracken must have thought, for he turned and looked back at me as if to ask, 'What does one do with these odd creatures about?'

I turned and walked away at right angles to the hare, Bracken swiftly arriving at my feet as if pleased I'd made the decision to move on. When I looked back the hare had gone. Hares do that, come and go, from and to unseen places; wonderful characters, truly as magical as the country lore that surrounds them.

From the creek road the spotted redshank was clearly visible, a little larger in appearance than the few redshanks near by, quite grey and with hints of the darker breeding plumage showing in the head and lower back. It was a lone bird, perhaps on passage but just possibly going to stay awhile, as they sometimes do here. A few years ago at Braunton Marshes I saw one swimming near a pair of shelduck, an unusual sight as one rarely sees waders swimming.

There are probably a few others about just now, flying in ones and twos on their way from their northern European breeding grounds to their central African breeding quarters. In flight the common redshank shows a white wingbar, whereas spotted redshanks do not, though both have the bright red legs or shanks.

At the top of the ivy-clad bank to the right of the creek road is a splash of colour amidst the green: the autumn leaves and bright pink fruits of spindle, a glorious sight. The ivy is in flower, an interesting way of ensuring pollination by insects with little or no competition from other plants. The countryside is still awake, though dozing off gently.

The old man's beard is a riot of silver, beautifully touched by the October sunlight. It cascades over the hedges to the wild music of the wading birds calling as the first tide tipples flow in along the creek mud, touching the feet of the dunlin who scamper before its soft coldness.

Shrill cries as the redshanks lift to fly northwards to the great river. Filling with tide from the sea and sending its waters to silver the creek, it lets the trees rest their reflections upon its surface.

On the border of Devon and Somerset impending storms, a black sky broken with shafts of light, created a luminous mood and with it an urgent sense of mystery. The antiquity of the landscape, deeply rural here where a long barrow speaks of ancient man, could be felt.

Rain had come almost as a surprise following the dry spell. Exmoor's streams were chattering again, lively, refreshed and refreshing as they made their secretive way along the coombes where the Doones once lived.

In a pool of swirling water, leaves and sticks spun, trapped, floating to the edge of the main stream then swung back again by the current until freed by more rain. Among the debris were a common field grasshopper and a crane-fly, both dead; picked up by the rains, they would eventually reach the sea coast, a last journey neither would have contemplated.

The grasshopper had probably hatched back in May. The females would have deposited egg pods in the soil and lived on a diet of grass in this lovely place, the songs of the males a joyous sound in summer. They will die now in October anyway, their job done, and their own young will hatch next spring. There are few insects lovelier or more of the summer than grasshoppers.

The crane-fly or daddy-long-legs is common enough, an autumn insect which will come into houses on autumn evenings, attracted by light. Their larvae, known as leatherjacks, eat plant roots and are themselves eaten by starlings and crow species in summer fields.

Splashes of rain warned of a soaking to come. Time to move on. I pondered on insect life picked up by vehicles and taken about. So many species are displaced in this way.

We stared for a long time at the object halfway up the old quarry face. It was a day of light drizzle, which is not funny if you permanently wear spectacles, as I have to do. The quarry face was a mixture of greys and greens, jagged scars with lines of stone forming wonderful shapes, craggy in places, soft in others where lichens grow. Disused for many years, the quarry was a good habitat for wildlife; such secluded places are virtually inaccessible to people and all the better for being overgrown.

The shape on the ledge moved slightly. It was a short-eared owl, most likely here for the winter but just possibly this was its home, for the habitat is right and I found long-eared owls breeding not so far from here some years ago. These owls hunt by low-level searching, in daylight or at dusk. The open ground adjoining the quarry provides ideal country, with voles and mice to be taken as food. A lovely bird, which we decided to leave peacefully enjoying its roost.

As we turned away, a hen bullfinch flew past us, followed by a cock bird. The hen vanishing into a tall holly tree as the cock dropped to the edge of a pool in the quarry, hopped in and began to splash-bathe. Ablutions over, the two flew high over the quarry edge and were gone. I had the feeling the bullfinches knew exactly what they were about, and had planned their visit to the quarry in order to bathe.

Homeward bound, water sunlight lighting the hips and haws along the hedgerows, soft greens and crimsons everywhere. Wild carrot umbels had formed into tiny bird's nest shapes. The advent of winter promised a wealth of good sightings and interest.

It must be National Mole Week. Seeing a mole in the wild is a rare moment, yet this week I've seen three, each one in daylight and in a different field. Odd that, or just good luck, for each time the sighting lasted less than a minute and then they were away. In the right place at the right time is the answer, but no way could I have judged that right moment. Us wuz three times blessed, me dearies.

Lovely characters, moles, with amazingly powerful forelimbs and smart velvety black coats. It is impossible for me to see one without recalling *The Wind in the Willows*. They spend a lot of their time breast-stroking through the ground beneath the surface from their base camp or fortress where they sleep and breed. Mole tunnels may be anything from just below the surface to about eight or nine inches deep, molehills being the surplus earth forced up. Nests are lined with dead leaves and used for both sleeping and to shelter the young. A main gallery leads off this chamber with other tunnels or corridors used for hunting branching from it.

Moles feed on earthworms, slugs and insect larvae, sometimes storing worms in a sort of larder.

Their original name was mouldiwarp (or earth-thrower), from the Old English *molde*, earth, and *warpen*, to throw. Lovely words. I must get out my old Devon shovel and warpen some molde about.

Old Bill, whom I sometimes bump into on my travels, used to catch moles, and my maternal grandfather was a mole- and rat-catcher as well as travelling with pony and trap to sell vegetables and fruit he grew.

If there is a spirit of the dawn, 'twas here all about us on this pale, wan morning which suddenly caught fire, warning of rains to come. The ribbon of a river turned to red from white in the few paces it took to reach and lean on a rail to watch the coming sunrise.

Curlew sounds bubbled across the mudflats. In a while, the ribbon of water would be a broad sheet of tideflow hitting the cutwaters of the bridge where the town is just awakening. A cormorant pointed its tail at the sky, diving for finger bass, leaving dark ripples in a ruby river already losing its colour.

The red sky had done its job of forecasting rain and took again the quieter pastel blues and creams. On the north-west horizon, however, dark clouds loomed like the spreading wings of the cormorants and crows who, knowing the tide would bring the rain, hurriedly broke their fast before fleeing the storm.

Rabbits cavorted in the flood meadow, chasing their tails as a wind sprang up, visible as it pressed the grasses of the saltings with its sighing passing, scented with the coming rain and salt smells from the sea.

Bracken rolled on his back, enjoying the freedom of the place, watched by the many gulls flying over. Their numbers have increased as expected, with the usual exciting surprises, such as over seventy great black-backed and thirty lesser black-backed gulls on the great ridge of sand and mud near Pottington.

Nearer Barnstaple, there were as usual a few common gulls and some herring and black-headed gulls. It is always worthwhile searching the flocks for the less common species of gull or wader.

Riverbank walk, soft underfoot, anglers enjoying a competition lined up along both sides of the river. About forty Canada geese and a few swans paid them scant attention as they glided up under Barnstaple Longbridge. Just here in the grounds of factory buildings we put up snipe from the saltings and were able to get close to two stonechats. They were a pair and will probably be about this area with its plentiful shelter and food for a while.

Six meadow pipits flew downstream as a kestrel hovered over us on beating wings. Bracken looked up as if to say, 'Don't even think about me for dinner' and trotted on, enjoying the scents of other life.

A large fellow in waders and white jumper clambered into an anchored boat and promptly fell off the other side. All was silence for a while and then he reappeared with a scowl, covered in river mud, staring at us with no humour whatsoever.

Along the footpath between factory buildings it always feels a bit grim but there is usually something to see. Today two black redstarts flitted away, over the wire mesh fence and into the area of concrete blocks and gravel piles. Had they not done so we might not have seen twenty or so pied wagtails roosting in the concrete yard against the blocks, because they were well camouflaged. Not a bad spot, for dark clouds hung ominously over the town, creeping in from Exmoor, making the old legs walk that much faster as we headed homewards along the Tarka Trail, where steam and then diesel trains once roared back and forth between Bideford and Ilfracombe.

Now the 'fast trains' to these places are streams of bicycles, the 'slow trains' the walkers, all enjoying the great outdoors, though not many will notice the snipe and stonechats.

Mild, raining and quite dark for the time of day, the lane running by the farm has every kind of grass and mud hummock imaginable and is all the lovelier for it. A shed built as a lean-to against a stone barn wall sheltered us from a sudden downpour and I wondered at the wildlife using this place over the years, for the building has been around for a while.

A stack of cardboard boxes stood against one wall, folded down and piled almost to the galvanised iron roof. Ideal habitat, this, for those primitive wingless insects we call silver-fish, which thrive on a diet of starch tissue including paper and glue, plant bulbs and other debris. Mainly nocturnal, they are probably best known to us from old books and such.

No doubt a queen wasp hides somewhere here, over-wintering, and centipedes, too. The window has curtains made by spiders, a few insects suspended in the misty webs.

A flutter of wings and four or five sparrows arrived, scolded us for being in their way and waited outside for us to go, perched in a tall holly growing by the door. Out into the lessening rain we went. I can take a hint; the sparrows mad it quite obvious that they preferred our room to our company.

Ahead of us, a crow fed from a rabbit carcass lying in the road at the lane's end. The rabbit had been killed by a passing vehicle and would provide food for carrion eaters.

Crows lead much more solitary lives than rooks and magpies. For example, the one nest in the leafless oak in the hedgerow is a crow's nest from this past summer. Quite possibly, it will be used next year by kestrels, for they do not build their own nests, of course.

Jasper, our tabby, crouched by the gate into the woods, watching squirrels who were scolding him non-stop. They saw him as a threat and hindrance to their obtaining nuts from the roof of top shed. He's not a squirrel-chaser at all, quite a home cat, but I felt he gained a perverse enjoyment from remaining where he was in order to annoy the squirrels. Cats have an odd sense of humour.

The name 'tabby', by the way, given to cats with the stripes and markings of or similar to a true wildcat, comes from an Arabic word, *attabiya,* meaning 'watered silk'. An apt name, methinks.

Jasper's whiskers are the longest I've seen on a cat and speak of his wild ancestry for, small as the wildcat is, it is a formidable hunting beast, its whiskers helpful in nocturnal hunting forays.

Quite a few mammals use whiskers as a means of knowing what is about in terms of obstacles and food; otters are a good example, as they often have to hunt fish in murky rather than clear waters. For the best use of whiskers, however, you do need a head in front and the rest of the body following behind.

Being a mammal and having a beard, I thought that in the interests of science I'd test this asset until, having walked into several things with my eyes closed, I decided to use the sense of sight again. What I do for science.

I found a small tortoiseshell butterfly hibernating in the bottom shed today. A touch faded-looking, but then so would I be if I'd been hanging up in a corner for several weeks. Hidden just around the corner are three primroses in flower, an absolute delight on this claggy day.

In this cold weather, food is in short supply for wild creatures; the seed-eating birds are likely to be better off than many species. Food and good plumage mean warmth, food being energy, and a lot of it is used to find more food. Diurnal birds, only having about nine hours of daylight, spend a lot of time food-searching between dawn and dusk.

Today a flock of long-tailed tits, ten or eleven of them, came piping through the woods. These are probably a family party wintering together, helping each other to find food and keeping warm at night by huddling together in a fluffy ball of flesh and feathers.

We were watching a greenshank splashing through the shallows after the tide had gone out when on the horizon over Heanton and Ashford large flocks of small birds, possibly fieldfares, darkened the sky momentarily like fast-moving clouds. Behind them, dark against the sky, came a small flock of swans, then more of the thrushes.

Under the stony bank where wheatears nest most summers, red dead-nettle showed pink snapdragon-like flowers, braving the winter winds; a pleasant surprise on such a day. Its Westcountry names are deafnettle, bumble-bee flower and archangel. I've known this plant to be covered in frost yet survive to flower on.

On the way home a quick look at the ladybird cluster discovered a while ago showed it is only about half the size it was previously. Whether they've huddled closer or some bird has taken a few I don't know. Of course, there has been frost, rain and wind to contend with as well as possible predators. We are fortunate to be human.

❖ ❖

Early this morning, I'd opened the top shed on the way out with Bracken, and fed and watered the birdlife and Grey, our squirrel. Coming back in a while later, around 8.30 am, I decided to peep into the shed through the window to see if any squirrels had ventured in for breakfast.

On the back wall are shelves, with gardening books on the top shelf, jars of nails and screws on the next, with twine and rope, and against both a long bamboo brought in from holding a sunflower in the summer. Some movement on the second shelf was a woodmouse, not too much of a surprise as they are always about. I watched as it went to the top of the bamboo, sniffed, touched it with its forepaws then, scrambling onto it, slid down backwards as on a fireman's pole, tail first. Into the nut sack it went, then scampered out and off with a peanut in its jaws. I waited to see what might happen next but the mouse did not reappear.

The woodmouse is found throughout the British Isles. It feeds on seeds, buds, fruits, snails, and arthropods, with some fungi, worms and even dead leaves. Breeding is from March to October, with good seed crops and warm weather often prolonging the season well into the winter. Young are born naked and blind and weaned by about eighteen days. Despite large numbers born mortality is high, small mammals having many predators including, increasingly, the domestic cat as well as owls, foxes, stoats, weasels and kestrels. Many die from taking in pesticides with food, including dressed grain, which they have been known to eat immediately it was drilled.

Woodmice display quite strong territorial behaviour, with both males and females defending their home areas against intruders.

❖ ❖

It is good to see tiny buds on the field maples again. I've planted a few for friends and it seems like only yesterday the leaves turned gold and fell to the ground.

I know we should not 'wish our lives away', as they say, but give me spring and summer any day. Anyway, looking forward to warmer times and favourite seasons has nothing to do with wishing one's life away; it's just about preferences. For me, spring and summer are dark chocolate; autumn and winter are milk chocolate. I like them both but prefer the dark stuff. Plain, like me.

Glancing at a water rail by the pool, I noticed a mound among the dead grasses that didn't look right, even though it was the same creamy colour. Binoculars showed the mound had eyes which were watching me, a female pheasant hiding, 'frozen' as the waters of the pool itself, darker markings showing now in the lovely plumage. Indeed, light and dark chocolate. A bird for all seasons.

The sky directly above was blue with grey mackerel clouds, the whole shading into the westerly sunset, deep rose colours with patches of apple green. A cormorant, jet black, flew powerfully across the redness which told of a fine day to come. The yammering of geese sounded from the river where unseen birds started up that almost frantic 'It's getting dark again' call which heralds the coming of night. Lovely.

Time to return home. Grey, our squirrel, was up and about awaiting his goodnight hug. A roast potato and a sweet chestnut for supper and into his cosy bed he scampered, well content, a couple of chestnuts put ready for his breakfast. Not a bad diet; better than chocolate, dark or light.

We stood in the field corner with only the roof of the farmstead in sight. The beech trees were here when I was a lad, I told my two younger companions. The field, now in grass for sheep pasture, held the spirits of farm labourers long gone. I used to come here at harvest time with my parents and other locals to pitch in at haymaking.

What memories: rabbits and field mice, voles galore, scores of wild mammals running everywhere as we helped or hindered. Then the sitting in the hedge as the farmer's wife brought food and drink. Back to work, happy voices, shouting, gradually stooks tied at the waist standing in rows, onto the carts and pulled to the farm. I've stood catching stooks and stacking them. I had the knack, I was told. Some stacked them too straight and down the rick would fall.

Standing in the field I saw it all, heard the 'ghosts' still laughing and working, then blinked to find I was back with my companions in the winter cold, talking of those days.

Machinery destroyed the closeness of people and such times even as it cut corners in terms of speed and efficiency, but that's progress in the human world. Swings and roundabouts.

There are old hedgerows here and bramble brakes with gorse, rich pastureland where buzzards soar and yellowhammers still prefer a cheese-free diet. The rabbits on the far hillside have come through myxomatosis and live with it now, nature deciding to intervene and help them through.

Good farming country this, where one feels the old spirit of the land means a great deal to the present farmers who, like the police, are now steeped in paperwork enough to fell half the trees in the countryside. Daft, ennit?

❖ ❦ ❖

I hadn't been back to the derelict cottage for some months, but during a visit to the area on another matter I made a brief detour. It was worthwhile in a way though it was a dismally grey and cold day. The ragged cotoneaster which seems to have a pact with the broken fence, in that they hold each other up, had tiny green leaves appearing. The gate I'd tied to stop it banging was laid flat now. Gates that are not upright seem sad somehow. I picked it up and rested it against a wall and, daftly romantic, I felt it gave out a happier aura altogether. And why not, I thought, patting it reassuringly.

The stone sundial has gone from its spot beneath the brambles and old roses. Although I looked around it was nowhere to be seen. It means there will be a new home for it somewhere, probably a good one if someone has gone to all the trouble to lift it out and take it away.

It's strange, that. Someone told me recently they had two of my hand-designed lampshades and, knowing the owner, I felt so pleased they had a good home. Inanimate they may be, like the sundial, but whoever makes a thing leaves some of their spirit energy within the make-up of the fabric.

The old shrubs here had been planted and tended by loving hands. Birds and insects will still be enjoying them this spring and summer and I expect there'll be a nest or two about.

I wondered what wildlife lives in what is left of the building but I didn't venture in. To scare creatures out into the winter's day is pointless and they may not go back in again. They are the occupiers, I the intruder.

In the pale light of evening, the two figures digging bait on the mudflats looked ghostlike as they bent to the task of seeking ragworms. Ragworms are both predators and scavengers, swimming with the aid of the many 'paddles' on their sinuous bodies. They may live in burrows or under stones and are called ragworms from their way of hanging limply when pulled from the mud.

Estuarine habitats are wonderful places to explore, ever-changing with the tide's ebb and flow, the light producing lovely pictures of shimmering, glistening scenes, the estuary birds and the flora of the saltmarshes always a joy.

And just close your eyes and listen. (Better stand still first, of course, or you'll be whelks over piddocks before you can say Jack Robinson.) Shelduck were laughing as they waddled landward; handsome birds now in breeding plumage after some time in 'eclipse', the moult plumage of late summer. The pairs hereabouts breed either in rabbit burrows, liking the local sand-dune systems, or occasionally in bramble brakes. There are some in the brambles just below the woods where we live.

Two ravens hurried south to some night destination, their deep calls telling of their lofty presence before we had seen them. At their courting and nest sites, their chatter is quite different: affectionate warblings and cooings, gentle sounds form these very loving and good-natured birds. But then we do so often tend to judge wild creatures as 'below' ourselves, when the truth is usually different. After all, digging up ragworms, who are probably quite happy with life, and using them as bait to catch fish could be construed as a cruel thing to do. Doesn't bear thinking about, does it?

Spring is rushing up fast; a lovely time. Three of us were in the rain by a swollen river where alder trees formed a natural corridor along its right bank, telling of the rich soil here. Once, much of lowland Britain would have had alder woods in valley swamps. Indeed, in the East Anglian fens one still finds dense alder woodland to remind us of those times.

Here, along the river, the trees are about thirty feet tall and popular with wildlife species as a source of food and shelter. The alder is our only cone-bearing broad-leaved deciduous tree and, now during the spring, is the time to look for its catkins, formed last summer in readiness for flowering during March and April.

A pair of mallards moved among the tree roots. They often nest along this bit of country, the alder trees being good shelter for them and the boggy ground keeping away too many people who may otherwise disturb their nest site. Mallard and alder are good friends, for the seeds that fall in the water are part of the diet of ducks.

Just a few weeks ago, after the freeze, we found otter footprints, called seals, along this very waterway. I know of three other holts in alder sites such as this one, all with underwater entrances protecting mother and cubs.

The alder is a very important tree to leave where it grows; a beautiful tree, and part of waterways, really. If man has to make a use of it, then excellent green and yellow dyes can be made from its catkins and young shoots, and a tawny red from its bark. And, of course, there is the pleasure of its being there to enhance the countryside, all a wise person would ask of a tree these days.

A woman with her young daughter and their dog stopped for a chat along the wood path. They had seen a thrush and been talking about snails and anvil stones used by song thrushes.

'When do slugs get their shells and become snails?' the girl asked me. I knew I was in for a long and involved natter, but first explained the fact that the two were different creatures and that there were numerous species of each.

A snail's shell is actually secreted by its mantle, a cloak of skin covering the body, and is made up of several layers. The snail first produces a thin, horny outer layer which is smooth and glossy, then deposits chalky layers on the inside. When the snail is fully grown the shell opening is strengthened by a thick rim. The shell provides protection against drying up as well as a partial defence against predators.

Except for occasional freak specimens the shell of each species coils in the same direction. Garden snails, for example, have the shell opening on the right, as you hold the snail facing you, so they have a dextral (right) coil. When the opening is on the left it is called sinistral. Complete coils are called whorls.

Snails lay eggs in shallow holes excavated in soil, laying from thirty to a hundred eggs. These hatch in three to four weeks, the young snails eating their eggshells to obtain lime for their own shell growth before beginning to feed on plants.

Young snails resemble the adults and have shells on hatching. Large snails take a year or so to mature and may live for two or three years, though some, such as the Roman snail, can live up to ten years.

So, fascinating creatures snails, well worth a closer look.

Spring Again

One solitary primrose in flower by Greenpool along with a patch of celandines. Though the leaden grey water reflecting a rainy sky looked bleak and forbidding, the flowers spoke of springtime and longer days to come. Frogspawn lay silent and unmoving against the bank, a living heap of eggs soon to be wriggling tadpoles. By then, the bank will be a mass of primroses and marsh marigolds which appear each year at the far end of Greenpool.

It is all happening, life burgeoning with the changing seasons; the natural continuity we know will occur, that we never doubt, is the very foundation of the faith of the ancients. It is a wise person today who makes it a part of his or her own foundation, for there is a deep lesson here for us all.

A pheasant called from near by and a moorhen answered. They knew Bracken and I were about, the wild sentinels communicating, even if it wasn't their intent but nature's way of safeguarding the living. I never cease to wonder at the pheasant's ability to avoid being seen despite its large size, though most creatures are adept at this when need arises.

Even dogs, I thought, as I stared about for a sign of Bracken. All was silent. He was in playful mood, waiting for a game. Along the bank, where rank grass formed pale hummocks just by a gorse bush ablaze with golden flowers, was the large black butterfly of Bracken's ears, often the giveaway as he lies watching in high grass waiting for a stick to be tossed.

Today I'd catch him out. I turned and ran to the kissing gates to hide under the trees. He was there waiting, bright-eyed, tongue lolling. 'Next game please,' his eyes said.

* ❀ *

Craig Rich had said it was going to rain. I had listened to his weather forecast and here it was, raining. Only I'd forgotten. It wasn't too bad under the trees, even without leaves on them. Only I was about two hundred yards from the trees. I could see Bracken keeping dry beneath them. He looked puzzled when I reached him, that 'Why didn't you keep up with me?' look.

Pressing back under the tree trunks, we watched the veil of water sweep downriver as we have done a thousand times before. And there, at the far end of a sort of tunnel of branches, perched upon a rock, was the first wheatear of the summer. A cock bird, he was quite the most splendid sight in his masked head plumage and smart grey and black with warm buff below. *Hwit-oers*, or white rumps; that's where the name wheatear comes from, good old Anglo-Saxon words living in our modern-day English.

They usually arrive in March as one of the earliest summer migrants, though one's ears tend to notice the chiffchaffs first. I've known them to nest and lay eggs as early as late March if the females have arrived. Well, it's difficult without the females. Eggs, that is. Usually April or May is the time for eggs and young, however. Do look for this species on the moors, heaths and coastal areas and listen for the 'whee-chat-chat' call that draws attention to its presence.

For birders keeping records of the more unusual species, we saw a great grey shrike on the afternoon of Sunday, 2 March. It was moving east to west along the hawthorns lining the Tarka Trail between Barnstaple and Bickington, on the south side of the River Taw.

* ❀ *

The silver of pussy willow, the female trees, in a row in the hedgebank while, as if in attendance, there's a male tree at each end of the row. These bear the yellow catkins, a familiar sight of springtime, as are those of hazel.

The hedgerow here overlooks a deep valley with a stream and across the stream, woodlands touched by a haze of pale green only visible when the sun is in the right place. By the water's edge are some fine purple willows growing as tall bushes around ten feet (three metres) in height. Willows are insect pollinated and so provide a lot for the wildlife enthusiast to observe, particularly the bumble-bees, who seem to have a special liking for willow. Indeed, the early supply of nectar and pollen is a magnet to bees and certain fly species.

A pair of marsh tits flew into the trees just across the stream, chasing about among sunlit branches, then dropping low to where primroses and a few wild daffodils basked in the warming sunshine. The marsh tits will nest in a tree hole, probably here in these secluded woods. The habitat is ideal with its mix of oak, ash and alder trees and good food availability. I once found a pair nesting in a gatepost holding a five-barred gate when there were plenty of trees about, so the hole in it must have been just right.

Marsh tits lay from five to eleven eggs, usually six to eight, which are lightly spotted with red-brown. Incubation takes about two weeks, and the fledgling period about sixteen to eighteen days. Usually just the one brood is raised each year.

To know more about Westcountry birdlife, join your county ornithological society and go on lots of field trips.

* ❀ *

I found a rusty old horse brass near a gateway. It had probably lain around for many years. It was a star or sun inside a crescent moon (depicting sun and moon worship), but the rust was so bad that it wouldn't clean up. However, it was an interesting find. It would have looked splendid shining on the mighty brow of a heavy horse.

These brasses derive from ancient Egyptian symbols and from Celtic, Roman and Saxon origins and such like and would have been worn as protection against evil and darkness. Good things, then, giving confidence to owners in the days when people were more aware of such matters – as some still are today, of course.

Different counties often had their own symbols and one can well imagine pixies being popular in the Westcountry, along with deer and oak leaves. Some are now collector's pieces and quite rare.

Looking across the field, we could see a few rabbits close to a warren hidden by brambles. One had a sizeable mouthful of grass, far too much to eat. The animal hopped to a burrow entrance and went inside. Probably a doe taking nest material into her nursery stop, a shallow burrow lined with grass, leaves and moss. The others suddenly scampered from sight. A moment later, two buzzards soared over, circled the area then flew off to the nearby woods. Maybe a rabbit had sounded a warning, though I hadn't heard it. The hawks would find other prey or maybe their next fly-past would be successful. A predator's life is a hit-or-miss affair.

A mole had been working the field edge; mounds of soil, the spoil heaps from shaft-digging, are a common sight.

They work hard, do moles. They say a mole can push 12 lb to 13 lb (6 kg) of soil in half an hour, which is well over fifty times its own weight. That's the equivalent of three tons of soil for a 10-stone (64-kg) person!

They are lovely creatures, and I suggest you sit by a hedge one day and watch the life of a field happen before your eyes. Who knows, you may see friend mole about his daily life. We are so used to our mole that it is difficult to believe that there are eleven species in the world that we know of, some, like the Mediterranean mole, smaller than our own.

As well as earthworms, moles eat a large number of beetle and fly larvae and slugs, the insect proportion increasing in summer and even more so in dry weather. The breeding season is March to May, so you may well observe more activity in the fields at this time of year, as well as in woodlands. Moles frequent lowland broad-leaved woods, though their 'hills' are not so easily observable in such habitats, of course.

I watched a water vole recently. Never thought it would become an endangered species in need of special protection. Here I was, watching a rarity, when once the gentle 'plop' as they dived into the water was a common sound.

Here we are in springtime, with all the glories of an English summer ahead of us. Fortunate are we, born or residing in the Westcountry, which surely cannot be bettered elsewhere as long as we share in the good custodianship of our heritage. Like the mole, we need to pull our weight and more in looking after the wildlife of countryside and garden.

In the green shade of oaks and hawthorn, the bank of the river curved in a sort of swan's neck. On the bend itself, the water is shallow, a deep pool opposite where water power has eroded the bank away. We had been told by a farmer where kingfishers were nesting and had been able to watch the last digging out of the new nest, the birds attacking the job with great vigour.

One couldn't have asked for better, for long-tailed tits were carrying feathers to a nest they were making in a bramble brake. How they find them, I do not know; over a thousand feathers to each nest. And there was another pair, building by the gateway of the next field.

The kingfishers' nest, a tunnel in the riverbank, is the perfect nest for their purposes and this one was nicely placed with branches out over the water and fishing pools with lazy currents near by.

'Summertime, and the livin' is easy, fish are jumpin'...'. The old song buzzed mellow through my mind but I didn't attempt to sing. Well, there were thrushes and blackbirds about and I didn't want them to be envious.

A great black bumble-bee hovered and zoomed along the riverbank. Bracken sat gazing at a mallard across the water where the bank was lit with primroses. One of the kingfishers flew by and I thought of the roads packed with holiday traffic people struggling homeward in their carbon monoxide world. Most of them probably have somewhere like this in walking distance from their homes. A simple field by a stream or river, a hedgerow and trees, the perfect base for nature-watching, never the same one day to the next.

Bracken rolled on his back, paws in the air. Luxury!

* ❀ *

For the past twenty-five years I've been making a study of a hedge, and can recommend it as a fascinating hobby and such a peaceful pursuit that doctors should suggest is as a stress-reliever.

There are always dunnocks in this bit of hedge. They are typical hedge-dwellers who rely on the habitat for shelter and food to a great extent. Just one pair holds this 100 metres of hedgerow as their territory, and I see there's another pair further on, so maybe 100 metres is about right to keep dunnocks happy and content. Of course, this same hedge is home for thousands of other animals and plants, man's own territorial behaviour and the keeping of livestock providing home situations and secluded highways for a wealth of species.

Just look for the well-worn runs of creatures in a hedge, used by hedgehogs, stoats, weasels and other small mammals, some at the top of the food chain. As Bill has said to me once or twice, 'Better to be a stoat then 'ees dinner.'

Even along the hedge bottom the worn pathway made by animals is quite marked, as they favour the shelter given by the hedge. Nests of birds and mammals are here, and the home of wasps and bees. Exciting places to be explored by the nature-watcher using eyes and ears.

I often see bank voles in 'my patch', lovely little creatures who seem to live at two speeds, either scuffling about in no hurry at all or moving like red-brown bullets along their runs. Today the primroses are blooming and yellow archangel is in flower. Ivy on a tree stump hides a brimstone butterfly from the cold wind, but at first warming of sun it'll be on the wing.

* ❀ *

In the greeny-gold glow cast by evening sunlight upon still water the grey wagtail watched me, her dark shining eyes unblinking, wary, for she had just built her nest here. Mossy green stones by the stream from a cavern were her chosen home, just where the swift-flowing water slows for brief moments to hush its chattering, to not wake her sleeping young, then passing by to chatter again over the shining stones beyond. Her young were as yet but thoughts in her tiny head and seed in the grey and yellow streamlined body.

Her mate perched ten paces away, bobbing his tail, watching her. He sang a thin, tree creeper-like song and they flitted together further upstream, fluttering up to catch midges which danced last dances over the water, or running along the shingle stones to take food my eyes could not see.

I touched the mossy stones, green velvet upon rock, firm living cushions that I stroked half a century ago when I watched grey wagtails nesting here.

Woodpecker drumming came loud from high in the woods as the dark brown shape of a buzzard flew, gliding among the trees at almost impossible speed. Then it upped its legs and wings to perch below the large stick nest over which protruded the tail of his mate, sitting in their green world in the canopy.

Bluebells among leafy trees, wood sorrel keeping them company. Various butterflies followed the pathway beneath the trees, flying from the wood edge to skip over the marsh-field. Great stitchwort climbed the grasses in full flower.

It doesn't get any better than this, I thought, and all for free – just as when I was a lad. Gosh, I was right when I was only ten!

* ❀ *

At 6.15, the woods were absolutely ringing with birdsong. The morning was grey, green and still. Dominant sounds were the calls of great tits, blackbird song and the gentler sound of warbler song overwhelmed by that of the resident species.

Bracken had gone on ahead, eagerly enjoying his early start to the day. Common and bush vetch were in flower and dog's mercury had been doing well since mid-April. There were rabbits scattered about the field and track, going about their business, one chinning its scent onto a gatepost, rubbing its head for a few seconds on the wood to mark it from a gland beneath its chin. It then stood on its hind legs looking about with twitching nose, selecting the smells it wanted which told its brain what was going on.

On the pathway the broken blue shell of a starling's egg showed where some predator had been at work, possibly another bird or squirrel. The starling's egg is clear blue though I have seen them almost white, but never with markings. Broken eggshells may not mean a marauder has taken them, of course. Birds discard shells after the young have hatched, but this was the egg of a hole-nesting bird well away from trees.

A hedgehog wandered across the path, sniffed at the shell and went on towards some daytime lair where it would sleep till nightfall. Generally nocturnal in habit, it's as late as I am early. Now that's a creature nothing like as common as was, and there's no doubt that habitat loss and vehicles have taken their toll of hedgehogs as well as a lot of other species.

But a skylark was singing in the distance. It was 7 am now and the Westcountry was well awake and on the move.

A walk along the beach is always a pleasant change, and to find several razorshells in the sand was a sought-after treat. 'Tis said the common razorshell is in serious decline due to overfishing. We're so used to picking up the empty shells of this fascinating creature, *Ensis ensis*, we forget it is but a part of a living sea animal. Razorshells have a lifespan of up to seven years or so and breed in the summer months. They live in deep, permanent, vertical burrows and speedily retreat down into these when disturbed.

One wonders at the terrible effect pollution must have on such lifeforms, unseen by most of us and thus often disregarded. We can understand or at least recognise the plight of skylarks and other farmland birds because their problems are visible; they are almost as conspicuous by their absence as by their presence.

Looking out to sea on this calm day it was hard to believe there were any problems as the blue-green waters lapped the shore, but did the gentle voice of the waves ask for help? Was the cry of a passing gull the crying of a bird whose ancestors were eaters of cleaner fish from cleaner waters? I think so.

A ringed plover scampered away ahead of us, dragging its wing in limping fashion. It was feigning injury in order to attract us away from four eggs laid among stones beneath a sheltering dune. What stress here, I wondered, as our large looming shadows and figures traipsed towards the fragile shells containing the beginnings of more ringed plovers. I for one breathed a sigh of relief that Mother Nature had imprinted the safety device in the brain of the little winged lady, for she must have screamed inside at our appearance.

Having safely detoured around the ringed plover's nest in the dune slack we went on between high dunes and along a track where a male stonechat told his mate of our presence. She'd be on eggs somewhere near by, as might the mate of the kestrel hovering in the distance. Both predators in their way, the stonechat possibly eating more prey species in a day than the kestrel will eat all year.

A bank of nettles grew fresh and spring-like as in the sunshine a solitary red admiral perched upon a leaf. We stood watching the insect on the food plant of its caterpillars; with its remedies for rheumatism, bronchitis, sore throats and asthma, a wonderful plant indeed. Thyme grew near rabbit burrows, a good antiseptic mouthwash and gargle source. Thyme taken with food helps the digestion. The rabbit smiling at us from the dune top looked pretty healthy, but then it would with such food all about. 'What's up, Doc?' would be about right!

A cock wheatear chased his mate along the top of a stone wall, on the other side of which lay marshy ground, miraculously holding water in places despite the serious lack of rainfall. Here a few red damselflies enjoyed the sunshine where a dyke stretched its way greenly across once-tidal land. The large red is a common species in the Westcountry and easily identified from its size and rich red colour. *Pyrrhosoma nymphula*, it is called. I know a few places where the small red can be found. Thank the gods they are tucked-away places, not at risk from development. If anywhere is safe these days, that is. Dragon and damselflies make for a fascinating study and there aren't that many species in Britain.

* ❀ *

Tree shadows fell across the river, reaching the little island with its few saplings of alder and some willow. Many of the trees never make it to full growth as the floods and storms every ten years or so rip them out. All the same, the island goes back to beyond my schooldays, for I used to sit there and watch the world go by during the summer holidays.

It is a grassy island with dock, plantain, some shepherd's purse and pink purslane. I've seen otter spraints on it over the years and many insect species, even grasshoppers which fly wind-blown from the fields on either side. Once I found a hedgehog standing on it looking at me as if to say, 'Now come on, get me off this place,' so I did. The creature must have been swept there by some spate and become marooned, a spiny Robinson Crusoe.

Patches of ragged robin, resembling red campion but with petals cut into four narrow lobes at the margin, ragged-looking indeed and very beautiful. It likes damp places and though mostly a rich pink, occasionally we find white flowers.

Equally attractive to insects is the marsh marigold or kingcups. Its brilliant gold shows now in damp places. Water forget-me-not with its delicate five-petalled flowers also grows here. This is the forget-me-not of water nymphs who surely live in such delightful places by streams and rivers.

From the tree shadows across the pool moved shadows that weren't solid yet ethereal to the eye: the brown trout, three of them together, nosing into water weeds near the island then on upstream to secret places.

* ❀ *

Further downstream from the little island, beloved of otters and other creatures, hemlock grew well on the bank of the waterway. Socrates drank poison from this very plant when sentenced to death in 399 BC; not a plant to toy with, but easily recognised and tall. I've seen it tower over me and I'm over six feet tall. It's a member of the carrot family, with parsley-like leaves, yet all of it is poisonous – seeds, roots, the lot.

Willow warblers had nested just between the wood edge and the stream bank, in a shady hollow where male ferns sent their fronds curving over the nest itself. The nest was low down, as is usual with the species, merging well with the vegetation. I'd not have found it had I not seen the birds at the site, having first heard the male singing, then the 'hooeet' call as the female flitted about.

They would soon have eggs if all went well; possibly five or six, which would take about a fortnight to incubate then another fortnight to fledging time. Usually one brood is raised a year.

I've found willow warblers nesting quite close to a pair of wood warblers a couple of times, once no more than a pace away, although there was ample habitat throughout the woods. That summer I was able to watch both species raise their young from a distance, a joyful two or three weeks with both broods fledging successfully. One of the countless great sightings of nature, a family of young birds flying into the countryside.

Some brown-lipped snails were carrying their colourful shells, orange with dark brown-marked spirals, along the dewy hedgerow. We counted seven as we wandered by. Then a song thrush appeared. Oh dear!

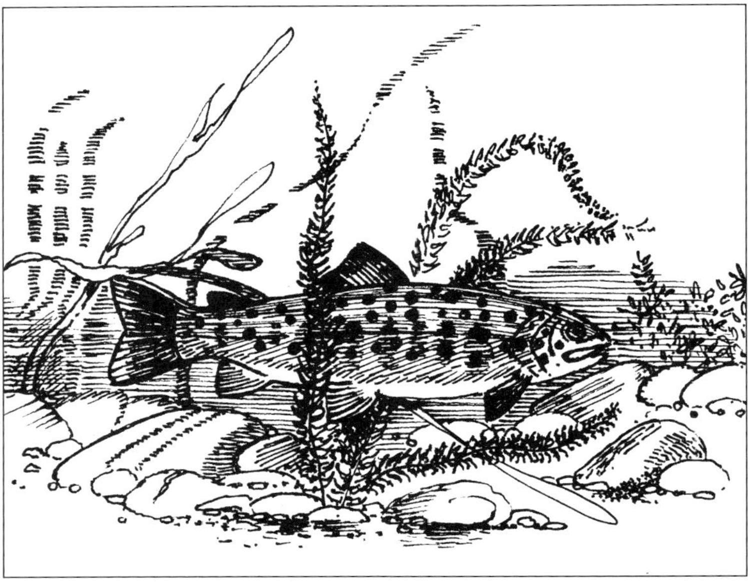

There is a bit of fencing in Anchor Woods, well enough made and put there to prevent people falling over what is unquestionably a nasty drop. Without even coming to take my measurements, the Council made it just the right height to lean on to gaze across the field to the river.

Looking north, song thrushes and rabbits feed in the field and beyond a few curlews probe the mudflats close to a cormorant standing with open wings like some gendarme directing avian traffic.

Below me on the steep bank held together by tree roots and other vegetation a great spotted woodpecker pecks away at old wood. I should have worn a hat. I watch spellbound for I haven't seen one of this species for ages, and he has no idea he is being overlooked. From my vantage point the scarlet nape is clearly visible, and he makes an almost comical picture as he batters away, pushing the powerful bill into the dead tree wood below, chips flying everywhere.

Somewhere in the wood below the woodpeckers could be nesting, for they should have eggs and even young by now. This male bird is probably seeking bark-boring beetles and their larvae. He gives me two or three minutes of sheer nature-watching delight, then flies west along the wood bottom.

Great spotted woodpeckers, like the lesser spotted, take ants, aphids and other insects, flies and such, but eat more vegetable matter than the smaller species, also taking fruit, berries, nuts and various seeds.

Ants and their pupae are a particular favourite of the green woodpecker, our largest species, who will take other insects and some berries and fruit. Lovely birds, woodpeckers; not as many about as there once were, though.

Third Summer

In a patch of nettles and dog roses, just along the lane, there are lots of dark brown bush crickets less than an inch long. They are out enjoying the sunshine at every opportunity and interesting to watch. Fortunately, they will be around until well into the autumn, possibly into November. Their pretty chirping song is an irregular sequence of short raspy chirrups. Walk in areas of rough vegetation on a summer evening and you may well hear them.

The wild rose patch here is wonderful, a sea of pink and some patches of white where field roses merge with dog roses. And the elder is just perfect this year, masses of white blossom with the lovely perfume drifting on the night air. It was so strong on the breeze that I took Bracken for a late night wander just to drink it in as a sort of last thing at night treat. How it lights up the darkness, the elder; millions of tiny flowerheads moving so gently, the pathway seeming to move for I cannot feel the breeze – well, only with my eyes, and with my sense of smell.

A reader has written to say she's bought some cassettes of birdsong and she listens to them in the garden after sunset, using earplugs and a personal cassette player so that the calls and songs do not disturb sleeping birds. She writes of honeysuckle scents, wind-tossed branches and the local tawny owls flying across the garden as she sits relaxed and watches the crescent moon rising, all to the sound of birdsong.

I might just try that. And it's a good point about not disturbing sleeping birds. They and other creatures have had a long day, often a hard day. Let them rest.

An old shed lay against the broken-down stone wall upon which a superb hedge had formed over many years. Just one window in the shed wall looking down over a valley and one pane of glass broken, the others being that 18-ounce glass used by picture-framers, held in more by luck than putty.

I had been given permission by the farmer owner to walk about the land. 'Go where you like,' he had said. 'There's little owls with chicks up in the old shed.'

Enough said, and here I was standing against a tree at thirty paces watching an adult and two young ones, both capable of flying. They were going cross-eyed watching bluebottles zooming about them. As if by some secret signal, out into the trees they flew to perch in a row on the low branch of an oak growing in the field amongst the nettles and wild roses.

The young were about six weeks old, flying well and keeping close to mum, who'd be teaching them how to catch insects, mainly beetles, and earthworms, molluscs and perhaps the occasional small mammal.

I moved against the tree. Immediately, the three owls began bobbing and neck-stretching to get a better view of this odd creature, but they remained together on their branch.

I wandered over to the shed, peering in at the window. Goodness, the owls had a table and chair, dust-covered, and two books lay on a shelf. Richmal Crompton 'William' books, both of them. I imagined the farmer growing up here: the perfect den, a wonderful view over the valley, watching the wildlife and reading a favourite book, climbing trees with his pals.

An old robin's nest rested on the shelf, the shed now a giant nestbox. A happy place, this.

A fox lay on the roof of the linhay in the sunshine – a splendid sight. Fast asleep it was, its own rich red conspicuous against the deeper reds of the old tiles and green moss. We'd been watching a buzzard flying along the valley bottom to answer the cries of its young, a scan with the binoculars picking up the fox way down below us in the next field.

Binoculars can take you to places where shanks's pony might disturb the best sightings. We were under trees, away from the bracken flies which can be a bit of a nuisance, and watching – nay, exploring – the whole valley from the one spot via our binoculars.

Hedge brown and meadow brown butterflies were all about, along with one or two skippers, while down by the river a dipper bobbed on a bankside stone. Another had gone downstream to seek the white-water shallows, for the June rains had raised the river levels. Where sheep grazed slowly along the field across the river, a grey heron arrived, dropping to the ground on outstretched wings to begin walking, peering into the pools as he went.

The berries of mountain ash were brown, ready to take on the scarlet of late summer. This, the rowan, is often found in hedges, the name probably coming from the Norse *runa*, for 'a charm'. As with the dog rose, the berries are rich in vitamin C and were once made into a scurvy-preventing drink. It is a lovely tree, but all trees are.

Good to see the hedgerows here well treed and not neat boxes, the tree and shrubs species bashed out of all recognition.

I glanced down at the linhay roof. The fox had gone, though we hadn't seen the going of it. Time for us to go too.

Watching a leaf-cutter bee at work is quite a privileged experience. This wonder of nature, quite similar to the honeybee in appearance, is an amazing insect. I watched one cutting away at willow leaves, quite precise ovals, using its jaws, and then off it went to a tunnel in the high bank. Luckily I was able to observe the insect going to and fro through the tunnel itself; being high up, I could only observe the comings and goings.

The little lady will take the leaf oval, roll it up into a cylinder, then seal off one end before stocking it with both pollen and nectar. Next an egg is laid and the remaining opening sealed with a circular lid of leaf. She will build a row of these capsules along the tunnel, which presumably has some light filtering in, for what a task it would be in darkness!

How the bees cut ovals and circles to fit so perfectly I can only imagine. They possibly use their bodies as a measure in some way, the limits of their minute legs and feet held apart perhaps. However they do it, they achieve what would be virtually impossible for us, but 'Needs must,' as we say.

We do not need to go back and forth long distances cutting out building material in this way; we have evolved a system of tools to measure, cut and produce. The bee, like other insects, is its own complete, amazing DIY system and worth observing closely at every chance.

This is an excellent time of year for bee-watching . The majority live solitary lives, unlike honey bees, who live a well-known social life. There are more than two hundred species of solitary bee in Britain, dependent on flowers and of major importance as plant pollinators.

In a rock pool about a dozen miles from where I live, we found some sea star coral, richly red and gold in colour, and some smaller yellow ones with yellow tentacles. Low tide had allowed us into an area of caves and gullies and it was like finding treasure beneath the water, the rich colours unexpected, lit by shafts of sunlight.

I didn't know what the coral was and had to find it in the books, but fortunately it was quite unmistakable, firmly affixed in solitary positions about the pool. The cave was silent, the only sounds the distant sea and the cries of gulls and jackdaws.

Magical places, these, but I am always wary of sea cliffs and caves, so attractive to youngsters on holiday yet always with an element of risk. Falling stones and incoming tides are ever-present in such places, so do take special care and warn youngsters of the hazards that are naturally mixed with the delights.

Green and brown shore crabs were about in the half-light, jolly creatures to watch, and there were either gobies or blennies swimming among the rocks and weed. Maybe there were both. I find it difficult to tell them apart just by watching them in the water.

Two adult oystercatchers walked by along the shoreline with a youngster in tow, not glancing our way, as a group of seven cormorants flew over the waves beyond them, no doubt intent on some fishing area near by.

Limpet-covered rocks were the perches of gulls, their calls the very essence of the seaside, while along the strandline sandhoppers skipped among the animal and plant debris searching for food. But there were plastic bottles and polystyrene, sharp tins and other nasties washed up. Please take the rubbish home.

A rainy wind turned the leaves over on the trees but behind the high hedge bordering a pool we were in shelter, a fallen tree making the perfect seat from which to observe wildlife. Moorhens were busy, some swimming, one or two young ones chasing about on the waterlily pads in the deep shade of rhododendrons at one end of the pool. As soon as I see them I think 'Dipchicks', for that's the old Westcountry name for them that I grew up with. A good name, too, watching them dipping and bobbing as so many water birds do, including dippers, wagtails and various waders.

We watched a spotted flycatcher flying out from its perch to catch insects, a lovely little bird that's always a joy to see.

'Look, there's a fly doing the same thing,' Endymion said, pointing to a clump of vegetation near by. It was a robber fly, a large fly with the lower part of its body as brightly yellow as the monkey musk in flower at the pond's edge. And indeed it was leaving its perch to catch tiny insects just as, in its own way, was the flycatcher.

Quite a few flies are carnivores, predators of other insect species; a number of flies have a go at us, of course, including mosquitoes, clegs and horse flies.

Common froghoppers were leaping from stem to stem on the grasses and wild flowers. The mottled adults are easily recognised, but may be better known from the larvae encased in 'cuckoo spit', the white, frothy exudation commonly seen on plants.

Just as we were saying what a good day it was for insect-watching, they started to disappear under leaves. A rushing of raindrops told us why. Time to go.

Like a slow-running rivulet of creamy white down a narrow creek, the flock of Exmoor sheep followed each other in single file along the track at the coombe bottom, silent save for the patter of their hooves. They then spread out in the morning sunshine to graze peacefully in this lovely place.

Brambles were bedecked with almost blown flowers, the green and red fruit a bit scraggy still but promising the birds an autumn larder. And the heathers were looking good.

It is a time for moorland walks. All is purple; even the spires of leaning foxgloves retain their glory to the last. They lean not with bowed spirit but with the contentment of seed about to be earthbound to bring forth next year's flowers. Nothing dies here; it changes form. It was from the earth and returns to the earth for the while, the one tall plant this year perhaps becoming a score next summer, or a few, or even one, but back 'twill come.

Pebbles of brown shone beneath the stream chattering over them. I knelt beside Bracken as he slaked his thirst. Brown, yes, but of many hues were the shining stones: red, orange, yellow, greens and blues, black and purple, grey, the curving arc of the stream making a rainbow of the stones, fragments of colour. Perhaps, like the foxglove returning to the earth, this is where rainbows go when the rain and sun and sky have done with them. Magic.

And by noon the trees at the lower end of the coombe quivered as a mirage with the heat haze, an unreal world. We moved on as people appeared on the upward horizon, our way being into the mirage, to where?